Making a
Winning
Short

Making a Winning Short

How to Write, Direct, Edit, and Produce a Short Film

Edmond Levy

AN OWL BOOK
HENRY HOLT AND COMPANY
NEW YORK

Henry Holt and Company, Inc.
Publishers since 1866
115 West 18th Street
New York, New York 10011

Henry Holt® is a registered
trademark of Henry Holt and Company, Inc.

Published in Canada by Fitzhenry & Whiteside Ltd.,
195 Allstate Parkway, Markham, Ontario L3R 4T8.

Library of Congress Cataloging-in-Publication Data
Levy, Edmond.
Making a winning short: how to write, direct, edit, and produce
a short film / Edmond Levy.—1st Owl book ed.
p.   cm. "An Owl book."
Includes bibliographical references and index.
1. Motion pictures—Production and direction. 2. Short films.
I. Title.
PN1995.9.P7L435   1994   94-6621
070.1'8—dc20   CIP

ISBN 0-8050-2680-0

Henry Holt books are available for special promotions and premiums.
For details contact: Director, Special Markets.

First Owl Book Edition—1994

Designed by Brian Mulligan

Printed in the United States of America
All first editions are printed on acid-free paper.∞
10 9 8 7 6 5 4 3

Grateful acknowledgment is made to Budd Schulberg for permission to use
excerpts from *On the Waterfront*, and to Andrew Wagner
for excerpts from *The Last Days of Hope and Time*.

This book is dedicated to
Denny Levy

Acknowledgments

I would like to acknowledge the astute suggestions and tireless dedication of my editor, Cynthia Vartan; the supportive comments from Professor Jorge Preloran of the University of California, Los Angeles, Professor Carol Bardosh of New York University, playwright A. R. Gurney, and Ross Lowell, who all reviewed the manuscript and were generous with their time. Other helpful readers were Kay Michaels, Jeremy Arnold, Jim Spione, Robert Bengston, and my students at Columbia University.

Special thanks to my research assistants Denny Levy, Leslie Holland, Carla Thompson, Rebecca Watson, and Jenny Bengston.

Contents

Making a Winning Short

Introduction

THANKSGIVING. After dinner. People are scraping off the remnants from their pie plates. I suggest to a half-dozen guests that they come with me to watch a short film. Nobody moves. They keep on talking. Finally, after the third invitation, six people reluctantly follow me into a room with a VCR. On the way, one person says, "I may not stay the whole time." Another says, "I'm supposed to be somewhere."

I have selected *Time Expired* by Danny Leiner. It's the story of Bobby, who returns home after a stretch in prison for stealing money from parking meters. He is cool to his wife and receives ardent phone calls from his prison cellmate, Ruby, a transvestite. With the passion of Bette Davis fighting for her man, Ruby uses every feminine wile ever tried. Bobby lies to his wife to account for his time with Ruby, and he lies to his lover about letting some time go by before they resume their relationship. Eventually, Ruby forces a showdown, and his passion prevails.

As the story unrolls, the remarks of my guests change. People are laughing. "This is much better than I thought it would be," says the one who warned me he had to leave. "Why can't we see things this good on TV?" asks an investment banker. The film has charm and candor. It is rooted in character truth and is funnier than the average sitcom with its quota of six to eight artificial laughs per minute. Unlike the sitcom, which is shot on one set, the short changes location. People laugh because the leading man never lets go of his working-class macho demeanor and his tough-guy New York accent. Everyone leaves with a smile.

More shorts are being made today than ever before, owing to the energy and enthusiasm of film students. I have seen their talent firsthand while teaching screenwriting at Columbia's School of General Studies. (My students come from Barnard, Columbia, the Graduate School of the Arts, and the working world of New York City.) Since it's hard to write a feature film in a term or even two terms, I recently decided to teach the short film instead. Everyone wrote much better once the goal became writing two ten-minute scripts or one twenty-minute script in a semester. There was even time for a revision or two, which is very necessary since economy of communication can only be achieved by revision. I have now changed the curriculum so that students are first assigned to write a ten-minute almost silent script called "75 words," in which students have to communicate their ideas visually. The next assignment is to write a twenty-minute short. Students are then asked to submit three premises (the unusual conditions on which the action of the film turns), which are read and discussed in class. Finally, the class and I come to agree on which is the best premise.

When developing this curriculum, I discovered that there was no book on shorts that I could recommend to my students and that nobody had tried to explain how short-making differs from other forms of filmmaking. There were books on making expensive movies and nighttime TV shows but none that addressed the practical concerns of the student or beginning filmmaker on a limited budget. To fill this gap, I decided to write a book that would cover all facets of the short film from the writing of the screenplay to production and postproduction.

My primary objective in *Making a Winning Short* is to pass on my knowledge of this medium to students as well as to beginning filmmakers and videomakers. I myself never went to film school full-time. I took night courses in television at American University in Washington, D.C., while serving in the Navy. I worked in the industry and managed to stumble into situations where I had opportunities to learn. I started by writing and directing shorts. The work was very hard, and there were no books or courses to guide me. But at that time, there was a great demand for shorts on TV, in theaters—where they were shown before the main feature—and in nontheatrical settings.

This is no longer the case. The markets for shorts on TV and in theaters have dried up in the United States. But this situation is not permanent. Nor is it universal. In Europe, the former USSR, India, and other countries, the short remains an entertainment staple. My secondary goal in this book is to champion this form, to survey its riches, and perhaps to create more distribution opportunities. We are exposed to so much repetitive material that we hunger for an offbeat story like *Time Expired*. Yet despite the fact that many excellent shorts are available today, they have been muscled out of theaters by promotional trailers. The more the distributors are worried about the acceptability of their films, the louder and more frantic the trailer. We are the poorer for it. Shorts can communicate a wealth of experience—beyond the marketing decisions that govern TV and most movies—and the good ones come from the heart.

Jorge Preloran, a film professor at the University of California, Los Angeles, thinks that student shorts reflect the changes in society in many ways. They deal with drug use, sexual preferences, the impact of divorce on children, new family styles and strategies, youthful unrest, the search for direction, feelings of isolation, feelings about parents, materialism, religion, new mores versus old, the loss of social guidelines, wariness about government. These shorts put a changing world under a microscope and come up with some valuable insights. If only the public could have access to them!

1

History
of the
Short

THE FIRST FILMS were silent shorts. Most films before World War I lasted from one to ten minutes, and the ten-minute film, or one-reeler, was the norm. In 1902, Georges Méliès, the French pioneer, made *A Trip To The Moon*, a film that still provokes laughter and pleasure. It is among the hundreds of shorts he created. The following year, the American Edwin S. Porter filmed *The Life of an American Fireman* and *The Great Train Robbery*, each lasting twelve minutes. These classic films were milestones in the development of the motion picture, and the latter opened our eyes to the power of crosscutting from one story to another.

After "talking pictures" were introduced, the length of feature films expanded, but the short remained a staple at movie theaters. In the thirties and forties, when a ticket to the movies cost ten to fifteen cents for kids, twenty-five cents for adults, the show included a newsreel, a cartoon, a short, a cliff-hanging serial, an "A" picture, coming attractions, and a "B" picture. The movie studios had total control over production and groomed writers and directors by having them first work in the shorts and B-picture units, the film schools of their day. In the shorts unit, the studios also experimented with color and film techniques. Some shorts had stars such as Robert Benchley, Edgar Kennedy, Pete Smith, and the Three Stooges. There were even musical shorts in which audiences could watch big bands that they knew only from radio. The cheers and applause at the end of a short often would dwarf the response to a feature film. In serial shorts, audiences saw familiar characters working themselves out of a different jam every week.

But the world changed. By the mid-forties, shorts began to disappear from theaters, only to reappear in the fifties and sixties when "art" houses began to flourish. Shorts and cartoons once again began to be a routine part of the movie bill.

When I arrived in New York in 1958, the czar of shorts was a man who always spliced in a title for himself—which read "George K. Arthur Presents"—at the beginning of each film he distributed. Arthur, a slight, short man (appropriately) who spoke with a high-pitched British accent, had in the silent era played dramatic roles under the name George Brest. In 1963, when I telephoned him to ask him to look at my short, he said, "Shorts should be as short as possible. How short is yours?" "Twenty-four minutes," I answered. "It's called *Happy Birthday to Me.*"

"Make it shorter, and I'll see it."

"I guess I could cut a couple of minutes."

"You should take out eight minutes. Don't recut the negative. Just cut the print."

"*Eight minutes!* I don't see how I could."

"Call me when it's ready." Click.

It may seem that he was tough and arbitrary, but, like most people in the film business, he was merely expressing the demands of his constituency—the theater managers who had to program films that would not compete with the main picture in terms of length or entertainment value.

It took me quite a while to pull seven of those eight minutes, which I had laboriously written, directed, and edited. I decided to lock in the length at seventeen minutes. The film was about a rarely employed but hopeful actress on her thirtieth birthday. On the screen we see the reality of her life, but on the sound track we hear the fantasies of fame that drive her dreams. When he saw my film, George K. Arthur would not distribute it because it was too long. Nevertheless, I took it to Hollywood, along with my pregnant wife and $1,000 borrowed from a bank against my car.

Making the film had drained all my savings. It had cost $13,000. Expenses were divided equally with my partner and cameraman, Richard Shore, the husband of Herma Shore, who played the lead. My talented sister, Kay Michaels, did the voice. In Hollywood, I finally found a mentor, Bruce Cohn Curtis, who got the film shown at Screen Gems, where studio chief Jackie Cooper gave me a job right after the baby was born. More about my firstborn, Jonathan, later.

Four years later I made a short called *A Year Towards Tomorrow*, which showed the adventures of VISTA workers. It won an Oscar and was distributed in theaters on a double bill with *The War Game*. I read later that it was seen by more people than most theatrical films. Profits reverted to the VISTA program, which sponsored the film. Winning the Oscar helped get *Happy Birthday to Me* into distribution. George K. Arthur saw it in a new light. Now he could advertise it as the work of an Oscar winner. Money started to trickle in, and when we sold the film to German TV we came very close to recouping our expenses over a six- to seven-year period.

Throughout the decades, a few attempts have been made to anthologize shorts into a feature-length film. In the fifties, three feature films based on stories by Somerset Maugham—*Trio*, *Quartet*, and *Encore*—were made in Britain and were quite popular. In the eighties, Canadian producer Rene Purlmutter brought out a feature consisting of shorts by women directors from around the world, and *New York Stories*, an anthology of three films directed by Martin Scorsese, Woody Allen, and Francis Ford Coppola, was distributed as a theatrical film. There is also in theatrical distribution a series of film school shorts by now-famous people called *Back to Film School*.

From the very beginning, TV was more successful with series than with shorts. For whereas a series offers the audience a familiar plot and predictable characters, a short is an unknown quantity; story line, characters, director—all are unknown to the viewer. Bernice Coe, of Coe Films, a leading distributor of the short film, sold shorts in the early fifties to *Omnibus*, the TV series hosted by Alistair Cooke. I also remember seeing *A Time Out of War* by Terry and Dennis Sanders, a narrative film about a temporary truce between two soldiers fighting on opposite sides in the American Civil War. In the seventies, when the cable era began, the short found a new niche in the entertainment landscape. Together with an HBO executive, Bernice Coe came up with the clever idea of filling the time between features with "interstitial" shorts so that movies could start on the hour, like network programs.

Although shorts rarely are used on American TV today, there are some notable exceptions. One outstanding program is *The Independents*, a series of shorts on the Discovery Channel. In this ongoing series, anchored by stars such as Paul Mazursky and Glenn Close, the theme changes every thirteen weeks. A recent theme concerned the female point of view, and all the selected shorts were directed by women; the series was hosted by actress-director Jodie Foster. In addition, Chanticleer, a progressive and talented Hollywood company, has been making a series of shorts for the Showtime network. (Many of these films are on my list of favorites in appendix II.) Another recent development is *America's Funniest Home Videos*. This TV series, which at one time was the top-rated show on the air, presents short nonprofessional videos submitted by viewers.

Outside the world of entertainment, there is an entire industry that uses the short film to sell everything from gasoline to safe sex to company policy. I myself have toiled in this field and made about sixty such films, many of them narrative. They are all intended to persuade the viewer to believe something or to do something (to stop smoking, to give money, to respect the United States), as opposed to the primary goal of most narrative films, which is to entertain.

One of the most prolific sources of narrative message films is the National Film Board of Canada. Since its founding in 1939, its mandate has been to make films that probe the history, politics, and social realities of Canada. It has won dozens of Oscars for live action and animated shorts, each of which fulfills the mandate but in a subtle and entertaining way. The U.S. government also funds films, though not as many as Canada. I have made some of my best shorts for the United States Information Agency (USIA), for the Office of Economic Opportunity, and for our armed forces. I made *Beyond Silence* (my first Oscar nominee), about a deaf girl going to Gallaudet College, for USIA. For the Office of Economic Opportunity, I wrote and directed three films, two of which were nominated for Oscars and one of which won.

The field of sponsored nontheatrical films currently employs 35,000 people, who make 1,500 films per year. Many of these filmmakers have other irons in the fire and make their living producing industrials, while squirreling away the money to develop their feature projects.

In fact, everyone who wants to create feature films begins by making a short. A short that is filmed to demonstrate one's talent, to raise money for a longer work, or to get a job in the film industry is dubbed a calling-card short. Directors Francis Ford Coppola, Milös Forman, Roman Polanski, Martin Scorsese, Steven Spielberg, Fred Zinnemann, Paul Newman, Susan Seidelman, Spike Lee, Randal Kleiser, and Robert Zemeckis all started out making a short. Many documentarians make the transition to film and TV with shorts. For instance, Ann Shanks made *Mousie Baby* to demonstrate her dramatic credentials and, as a result, got a directing assignment for a TV movie. She went on to produce several successful TV movies.

Despite the fact that the market for shorts is diminishing in the United States, more short films than ever are being produced by students in film schools and by amateurs wanting to explore their talents with the video camera. According to Richard Ross, former head of the New York University graduate film program and previously head of the Columbia Graduate School of Film, Columbia graduate students spend 68 percent of their time on shorts. (Unfortunately, they received no instruction in the subject until recently, when playwright and TV writer Corrinne Jacker began to teach the short film.) Ross says that at NYU alone almost 4,000 shorts are produced annually, making the school the largest 16mm customer in the United States.

The appeal of shorts is understandable. They are not interrupted by commercials, and they are fun to view. Shorts made by young filmmakers who are not inured to commercial standards are often fresher than the formulaic series on TV. Although the rules for shorts are not as stringent as those for features or series TV, certain rules of dramatic writing still apply, as I will show in the chapters ahead.

2

■■■■■■■■■■■■■■

Defining
the
Short

HOW SHORT IS A SHORT ANYWAY? The Academy of Motion
Picture Arts and Sciences says that shorts should be less than
thirty minutes. To sell your short to TV, you must keep its length
under twenty-four minutes. If you want to make a calling-card
short to show off your talent, fifteen minutes or slightly less is the
ideal length. Adam Davidson's film *The Lunch Date*, which won
the Grand Prix at Cannes and an Academy Award, was only eleven
minutes long. The last minute packs a wallop and makes the film
resonate in the mind over and over.

Just as the length of a short is flexible, so, too, are the rules
about its structure. Whereas all full-length feature films follow
more or less the rules laid out by Robert McKee in his lectures and
by Syd Field in his basic text *Screenplay*, the short dispenses with
some of these structural mandates. (I'll be discussing the rules
that do apply to shorts throughout this book.)

Shorts tend to be highly visual. They are closer to feature films
than TV shows in the sense that more action is portrayed on the

11

screen and the storytelling relies more on images than on dialogue. People in Hollywood prefer shorts with silent passages, so
you will get farther in your search for financing or a job if you can
incorporate such passages in your own work. This preference
stems from the film industry's reverence for the silent-film classics
in which everything is communicated through the characters'
behavior, the camera, and the editing.

One of the best examples of a silent short with a contemporary
score is *Skater Dater*, written, directed, and edited by Noel Black.
Not a word is spoken in this exquisite film, which shows one boy's
breakaway from the camaraderie of a skateboarding club to begin
dating a girl on a bike. Filmmaker Black retains motion as his
filmic vocabulary. Instead of Girl Meets Boy, it's Girl Collides
with Boy, she on a bike (a mode of transportation more suited to
courtship than the male-conformist activity of skateboarding in
unison). The film was nominated for an Academy Award.

Many shorts have surprise endings, which make them highly
memorable. Two consummate masters of the switcheroo ending
were Guy de Maupassant and O. Henry, whose short stories finish
with a sudden unexpected twist to the plot. An effective short
based on one of O. Henry's stories is *Chaparall Prince*, in which
overworked Lena writes to the mother she ran away from about
her slave-labor conditions. The stagecoach carrying her letter is
robbed. One of the robbers reads her letter and rescues her. Closely
related to surprise endings are false resolutions, which seem to end
the film on an unsatisfactory note; they pave the way for the real
ending, which comes as a relief and a surprise.

For the filmmaker, using a well-known short story or novel can
cut both ways. On the one hand, you don't have to come up with
your own story line, but on the other, you risk alienating the
public if you put your own stamp on the film by changing names

or aspects of the plot. Nevertheless, some successful TV series have been based on short stories: *The American Short Story* on public TV and *The Ray Bradbury Theatre* are two examples; the Maugham stories have already been mentioned. Among the recently made films from short stories are *Greasey Lake*, from the story by T. Coraghesson Boyle, and *The Fifteenth Phase of the Moon*, based on a story by Celia Roebuck Reed.

Now that we have touched on some of the general characteristics of shorts, let's turn our attention to the main categories in which shorts tend to fall. I came up with seven major categories of shorts after viewing such films over a two-year period and consulting with those in the know: film teachers at New York University, Columbia University, the University of Southern California, and the University of California at Los Angeles; distributors such as Tapestry, Coe, Phoenix, and Pyramid; and producers such as the American Film Institute, Chanticleer, and Atlantis. The classifications are arbitrary, not infallible, and many shorts belong in more than one category. The following sections include descriptions of each category and illustrative examples. (For complete synopses of the shorts referred to and information on their distributors, see appendix II.) When reading this material, bear in mind that each successful short has a premise, an assumption the audience is asked to believe, which forms the basis of the story. In the short *Board and Care*, for example, the premise is that retarded teenagers have normal sexual longings.

Science-Fiction Shorts

These shorts are like the science-fiction genre of fiction in which an imaginary world mimics scientific developments, such as cloning *(Jurassic Park)* or robots *(Robocop)*, and turns a scientific speculation into an assumed reality. In short films, there is no budget for special effects, but there are less expensive ways of creating a different world that reflects timeless truths.

The sci-fi short *12:01* shows an inhibited man, on poor terms with the world, who has held the same job for twenty-three years. He suddenly finds himself repeating the same hour of his life until he realizes he can enjoy the recurring events and change some of them. The film was nominated for an Oscar, and the premise was turned into a feature film called *Groundhog Day*, starring Bill Murray, and into a TV movie.

Another sci-fi premise is contained in *Kaboom*, directed by Gabrielle Luzzi. A man brings home a nuclear bomb as a novelty fad item. At first his wife is worried; then she treats it like a baby, and the dog plays with it. Neighbors drop in to admire the bomb, but soon they want their own, and finally, the fad becomes a threat.

Metaphorical Shorts

A metaphor is a way of showing reality by an invented comparison. In the novella *Metamorphosis*, for example, Franz Kafka's character of Gregor wakes up as a giant cockroach and proves an embarrassment to his family, just as in real life Kafka's writing brought shame to his conventional family.

Two metaphorical shorts that are highly effective are *Welcome to I.A.* and *Ray's Heterosexual Dance Hall*. In *Welcome to I.A.*, no one hears what Paul is saying at his birthday party. He realizes he is having another attack of invisibility. Paul joins Invisibles Anonymous where he learns that when *you* start seeing other people, *they* start seeing you. *Ray's Heterosexual Dance Hall* is a parody of male bonding. Businessmen court financial relationships as they seek out men as dancing partners. Dancing is a metaphor for romancing deals.

Fantasies

A fantasy is an imagined world that serves, like a pleasant dream, to resolve human pain. Intolerable reality can be corrected in a fantasy. In *The Room*, a boy of ten is held captive in his apartment by a tyrannical father. The boy fantasizes that his bed blasts off from the apartment like a spaceship and gently lands in the street below, where he is warmly greeted by neighbors. A similar film is *End of the Rainbow*, which shows a depressed, untalented musician playing his saxophone badly on his fire escape. When jeered from below, he jumps to the street. The fantasy locks in: He staggers to his feet. A woman hands him a sax, which he plays brilliantly, and the whole street joins in a wild musical number. When the film returns to reality, the street becomes deserted and the man lies dead on the cold pavement.

With Hands Up takes its inspiration from a famous photograph snapped by a German photographer during World War II. The subject is an eight-year-old child in a newsboy hat, the picture of innocence, who has his hands up while being herded by the Nazis. When the wind blows his hat off, he chases it out of view to freedom. *The Howie Rubin Story* is about a young man who is an underachiever except in his fantasies, where he is admired by girls and interviewed on a major TV show about his life.

In *An Occurrence at Owl Creek Bridge*, a man fantasizes about idyllic happiness in the few seconds he has remaining while dropping from the bridge with a noose around his neck.

Anthropomorphic Fantasies

A related type of short endows animals or even a balloon or a chair with human qualities. In *The Red Balloon*, a film by Albert Lamorisse, a balloon bonds with a boy like a pet. When bullies puncture it, the boy is rescued and carried off by a whole bunch of balloons. *A Chairy Tale*, about a chair that takes on a life of its own, belongs in this category, as does *White Mane*, another Lamorisse film that features a free-spirited horse who escapes capture with the help of children. *The Dog Ate It*, discussed in chapter 5, also qualifies as an anthropomorphic short.

Character Development

In this genre, a protagonist is revealed or changed after being tested. In *The Bet*, we gradually see how insatiable and self-destructive is the addiction that grips a compulsive gambler. In *Sandino Bambino*, a bookish idealist does not realize the price he pays for being oblivious to reality until his father runs off with his girlfriend.

Sometimes a character undergoes a change after being caught in a crunch between value systems. In shorts about immigrants, for example, old-country values and American values are often at odds. Carolina in *The Fifteenth Phase of the Moon* is torn between her parents' Mexican values and her strivings as an artist and a first-generation American woman. With her mother's help, she is able to leave home. The Russian émigré writer in *The Laureate* learns to give up his past struggles in Russia and to seek happiness in America. There is a cultural conflict of another sort in *Halmani* when a Korean grandmother and her granddaughter have clashing values.

Character can also be developed through an odd-couple relationship. In *Night Movie*, an Israeli soldier bonds with and trusts an Arab captive, who is later rashly shot by his fellow soldiers. In *Graffiti*, a young artist cleverly tweaks the military dictatorship of his country with his graffiti until he sees a young woman who does similar drawings being carried off to be tortured.

Character change often involves giving up something that holds you back. In *The Last Days of Hope and Time*, a man who was almost but not quite recruited by major basketball teams has to give up the dream that keeps him on the basketball court in the park. Characters also change when they defy society. The lead in *Birch Street Gym* joins a boxing club for senior citizens and boxes even when everyone in his retirement home urges him to be sedentary.

Rites of Passage/Memoirs

A rite of passage is a highly charged experience in the life cycle, such as realizing that parents are not perfect, discovering self-worth, being in love for the first time, having a first child, growing older. On film, these experiences are usually portrayed in a warm and sentimental manner, which suits those in the audience who have already gone through them. Seeing a rite of passage depicted on the screen may be painful, however, to the person who is currently undergoing that experience. Other autobiographical material also falls under this heading. For example, the short *Portrait of Grandpa Doc* remembers the warm, gentle mentor of the filmmaker's childhood. In *Tell Me*, two girls promise to go through puberty together, telling each other everything from the first kiss on. But one develops breasts before the other, spoiling the bond. In *How Sticky My Fingers, How Fleet My Feet*, men in their thirties face the decline of their physical strength when playing touch football in the park with a sixteen-year-old.

Parodies

There are roughly two kinds of spoofs—critical and reverent. *Day of the Painter* is a critical spoof about people who profit from facile modern art. *The Dove*, on the other hand, is a reverent satire of Ingmar Bergman's movies, made when he was the world's leading film artist. Bergman's cameraman, Sven Nykvist, told me that Bergman saw the film unexpectedly in a theater and was practically on the floor laughing. He has since bought a copy and plays it frequently. *Missing Parents* is about runaway parents who find a shelter for abused parents—a satirical switch on missing children.

3

Starting the Script

Getting the Idea

Wisps of gossamer float in the mind—fallout from childhood memories, haunting passages from books, movie scenes that we rerun on our inner screen, things we remember, things we heard. The writer collects these shiny filaments and twists them together into threads, then weaves the threads into a tapestry which is the script.

The best shorts reveal pungent truths that grow out of the filmmaker's personal experience of living. The trick is to get in touch with what you already know, to trust your instincts, and to allow your writing to expand beyond the literal truth; then you must look at your script with a critical eye, revise as necessary, and expose it to the slings and arrows of your friends and colleagues.

Have you ever experienced something and wished you had a camera because you knew nobody would believe you? Have you held people spellbound when telling a particular anecdote from your life? Maybe you have told a story at a bar or a party, and the laughter kept on rolling. The seed of a film script often lies in these situations. In a short narrative film, you can build a story around a core of truth. You can edit and shape your material in any number of ways. It is simply a matter of writing up the event or encounter, showing a set of fictional causes, and persuading the audience to believe the story as it unrolls on the screen.

Draw Ideas from a Journal

"I bruise easily. And when I bruise . . . I write," said S. J. Perelman, our greatest modern humorist. Like Perelman, you can record your own bruises, distasteful encounters, and frustrations. Write down in a journal the witty ripostes you make to yourself once it's too late to attack the person who has insulted you. If you're like me, you rewrite your verbal swordplay after you have been trounced in an actual exchange. But in the *rewrite* of the dialogue with loud drivers and brusque officials, we come away clear winners. And we can hone our unspoken dialogue long after the confrontation. Similarly, a script for a short is the chance to correct the sloppiness of everyday life with brilliant afterthoughts.

Three Ideas for Shorts

I think of how frisky my VCR is. I set it carefully, looking from the monitor to the instruction book, trust that I am ready to record programs, and something happens. All the instructions are erased. Maybe there is an idea for a short here: a man finds that his electrical appliances are rebelling against him. The toaster burns his toast. The water purifier turns his water brown. He sets the VCR to a football game, but it records a sermon.

A favorite story comes to mind that began on Thanksgiving, 1968. It concerns my son, Jonathan, the one who was born in Hollywood right after I moved there to further my film career. It's four years later. I am divorced, living in New York and frequently working in Washington. I have a second son who's three years old, a year younger than Jonathan. I take the boys to a family party on Thanksgiving so they can meet their cousin Peter from Washington. Compared to his self-confident cousin, Jonathan seems shy. He grabs my leg, peeks at Peter, and says nothing. When Peter speaks to him, he stares at the floor.

"What's a cousin?" asks Jonathan later.

"He's like a brother, but you don't have to live with him." That seemed like found treasure to young Jonathan, already burdened by living with a competitive younger brother. For two months, Jonathan talked of nothing but Peter.

Then, in February of 1969, Jonathan had a chance to see Peter again. I was scheduled to be in Washington for two events. One was the showing of a new film on a neighborhood health center for a senatorial committee. After that, I had to direct a crew at a press conference with the vice president. I invited Jonathan to come along with me on the trip. My cousin Linda promised to meet us at the Washington airport and care for Jonathan while I attended to business. But when we got on the plane at La Guardia, it developed a flat tire and the flight was delayed; by the time we reached Washington, Linda had given up and left the airport.

My heart pounded as we rode to the Senate building. The

screening would be over by the time we got there, but maybe the crowd would linger so I could get the senators' reactions. I told Jonathan that I didn't want him to act like a baby; that we were going to be with very important senators who pass all the laws and who wanted children to be quiet while they talked business.

When we got out of the taxi, he refused to take my hand and follow me.

"Carry me," he said.

"*Carry* you? Why?"

"I'm afraid the men won't like me." As I carried him up three flights of marble stairs, I wished I hadn't intimidated him.

Huffing and puffing, I arrived at the committee room, with Jonathan still in my arms, expecting the film to be over. It had not even started. Several aides were clustered around the projector. By the time they got it working, I had to leave for the White House. What to do with Jonathan? I spied a woman who was the central character of the film, a poor woman who had probably never been outside Denver since she and her husband had eloped there from Mexico. The committee had flown her in for the screening. I asked this woman, Maria Guzman, if she would watch my child. She hesitatingly agreed. I gave her Linda's phone number, she gave me the number of her boardinghouse, and I gave Jonathan money for taxis.

I went to the White House, got my cameraman a good position, waited for the press conference to end, and then dashed to one of those press phones where reporters call in their stories. I reached Maria Guzman, who said, to my amazement, that Jonathan had taken charge of everything. Before he got into a cab, he checked all the tires so the same morning mishap would not recur. He told the driver that his father was at the White House, so they had better not get lost. When they arrived at the boardinghouse, he handled the fare and the tip. After all, he was a seasoned New Yorker and Maria Guzman never took cabs in Denver.

Once at Maria's, he kept calling Linda until he reached her at home; then he called a taxi and had Maria copy down the cab's number. As the cab pulled away, Maria could hear Jonathan telling the driver that his father was with the vice president. Later, when I met the boys and Linda in front of the White House, the cousins were chasing each other. Clearly, Jonathan had emerged from his shell and come into his own. On the plane back we both breathed a sigh of relief as he fell asleep against me.

Another experience. Recently I went to a blood center for tests ordered by my doctor. Something about the place was askew. It was in a seedy brownstone. The sign on the door had letters missing: "Un ed Me c l T st g." Another sign said to ring the bell to be buzzed in, but after several rings the door never opened. Eventually, someone exited, and I snuck in. The receptionist was on the phone speaking aggressively in a German accent. When she was finished, she told me to sign a sheet. I tried to tell her that I had forgotten to bring along my doctor's instructions but he could be reached by phone. She seemed unable to process this information and told me to wait. Finally, she called my name and asked for my doctor's instructions. I again told her I had forgotten them and said she could call his office and find out the tests he wanted me to take.

"What's his number?" she asked.

I gave his name and street address.

"How can I call him if you don't give me his number?"

"You could look it up in the phone book if you knew how," I said, getting up to leave. I had been there twenty minutes by now. "You're stupid," I continued unnecessarily.

"So are you. You forgot the instructions."

Unfortunately, she had the last word. I *was* forgetful. Unsatisfying. Real life. As I walked away, I thought of some good lines. I should have said, "If you are paid to drive patients away, you are earning your pay. But if you are paid to be helpful, you should be embarrassed to take money." And I thought to myself, "When I get home to my journal, *I* can have the last word. I can have the consolation of correcting reality by writing a scene in which I am beyond reproach and uncover a nest of bullies." The slow-witted writer can wreak revenge by amending the record—and expanding it. An idea for a short emerges. . . .

A man enters the lab office, somewhat flustered, to get a test. He encounters a military-style woman who speaks with a German accent. Wagner plays on the tape, and a male attendant distributes German periodicals. The man fills out a form and shows it to the receptionist, who cross-examines him Nazi style as if he is hiding the truth, then commands him to sit and wait. From one of the examining rooms come blood-curdling screams. Our hero looks around and finds that no one else seems to have heard anything. Another scream. And another. In the back offices, some Nazi doctors are continuing experiments in human endurance started during World War II.

But then I get uncomfortable with the fact that my short is attacking Nazism, an old stalking-horse in film, with nothing new to say. It's like being against sin. Perhaps the point worth making is that Nazism can resurface where we least expect it. Maybe I'll drop the guttural and staccato German accents in favor of charming French accents, or crisp and coolly British accents, or even corn-fed American accents. I think of David Duke, the candidate for governor with a Nazi and KKK past, who now sits in the Louisiana state legislature. He's not wild-eyed. Nor was Senator Joseph McCarthy. Evil, as Hannah Arendt taught us, can appear in a banal form.

Finding the Premise

Many people start by asking "What if?" and then they create characters that go with the premise. Canadian experimental film-maker Norman McLaren asked the question "What if a chair had feelings and moods?" In his *A Chairy Tale* a chair takes on a life of its own, teasing and tormenting a man who wants to sit down by continuously eluding him. When he decides to spurn the chair, it pays court to him and begins to act like a pet, jumping on him. The chair reminds me of a dog with a bone. When you try to take a bone from its mouth, you get resistance. When you give up, the dog pursues you and tries to give you the bone or any form of love you will accept.

You often arrive at this kind of premise when you see something that everyone accepts as normal even though it isn't. Example: A man living on the street is spread out on the sidewalk outside Tiffany's in New York. People step over his body and keep going. The camera zooms to the sleeping face, then goes out of focus to indicate "What if." A businessman is about to step over the protagonist but recognizes him as an old high school friend, wakes him up, takes him for coffee, recalls old times, brings him home, cleans him up, and takes him to a high school reunion where he sees his old flame. She confesses that she always loved him. They swim in the high school pool, make love in the chem lab. The woman asks him about his life after high school. He describes how everything went well until two of his classmates died in a car crash while he was driving. . . . We switch to the more likely scenario. The businessman steps over the man on the sidewalk and then says, "By any chance did you go to high school in Morristown?" Our protagonist shakes his head and goes back to sleep.

What if a mediocre singer bought a bird that sang better than she did? Phyllis Raphael used this premise in a short story, and William Chartoff made it into a short called *Duet*. What if a highly developed robot could destroy a man's confidence because the robot always had a better idea? And consider these premises:

A homeless man wants a nostalgic dinner date with a homeless woman. *(Sunday Dinner)*
A heterosexual dance hall exists where men dance together and make business deals. *(Ray's Heterosexual Dance Hall)*
A high school holds plumbers, not athletes, in high esteem. *(Aisle Six)*
A man threatens to ignite himself if his girlfriend does not take him back. *(That Burning Question)*

In the end, the premise may be the most important aspect of the film. Any short can be well acted, well directed, and well edited, but what really distinguishes the film is the concept. Is it something we have never seen before? Something delightful, wise, thrilling, refreshing? It is a good practice to come up with two or three short ideas before you plunge into the screenplay. See if people are more receptive to one than the others. If the ideas are received equally, make your own choice and put the others aside.

How to Create Character Profiles

Do you believe that character is destiny? I do. And most drama-
tists do—at least when they write. Why else do psychiatrists
point out that we make the same kinds of mistakes over and over
again? Or fall in love with the same type of person over and over
again? Many films are about an attempt to change the unconscious
script. For example, a third-generation fireman takes reckless
chances to compete with his highly decorated but dead hero-
father. His moral character might compel him to follow his
father's script and perish. But then he marries a woman with a
different agenda. She convinces him to make a 180-degree
change. He becomes a cautious insurance salesman, who carries a
briefcase, dresses to avoid criticism, and assesses risks.

One day he happens upon a burning building and rescues some
people before the fire trucks arrive. The firemen greet him
warmly. Someone hands him his briefcase but he throws it in the
trash and rides back to the station with his buddies. Character is
destiny.

Once you have a premise, find a character whose experience will
demonstrate it. But allow the character to breathe, to be a whole
person with faults, virtues, and unique qualities. Explore your
character. Henrik Ibsen, the great Norwegian dramatist, used to
start his plays by interviewing his characters. They were the only
company he needed while he was getting to know them. I recommend filling out the accompanying form which I developed for
my students as a way of interviewing your characters and deriving
your plot from their traits.

Character Profile

How to Use This Form: Make photocopies of this form so you can create a separate profile for each character in your screenplay. When you start writing, fill in as much information as you can. As you work on the scenes, add any new character information generated by those scenes. If you get stuck at any stage of the writing process, come back to these pages and start expanding on some of the categories. The exercise may get you back on track.

Age:

Main Trait:

Humanizing Trait:

Profession:

Address:

Values:

Foil:

Obsession:

Goal:

Idol:

Epitaph:

Internal Conflicts:

Interpersonal Conflicts:

Societal and Environmental Conflicts:

Best Thing That Could Happen to This Character (which could turn out to be the worst):

Worst Thing That Could Happen to This Character (which could turn out to be the best):

Why the Audience Will Root for This Character:

Voice (a description of the inciting incident that kicks off the drama, from the viewpoint of the character):

Let's go through the items on this form one by one.

Age: I don't necessarily mean chronological age, although this can sometimes help us understand a character, as in the 1991 movie *Frankie and Johnnie* where Frankie increases the age she admits to Johnnie as she trusts him more. Mostly, I mean developmental age, that is, the stage of life the character is in. For instance, if the character is male, is he past college age but not yet committed to a career path? A good reference while you're writing your screenplay is Gail Sheehy's book *Passages*. She has popularized the work of Erik Erikson, who studied the challenges of each developmental stage.

Our task in probing character is to find external equivalents to inner states so that we can *show, not tell*—which is the secret of good filmmaking. Let's say the character is a woman lawyer, thirty-five years old, and her biological clock is ticking. She wants to have a baby, but Mr. Right has not shown up. How do we show she's in conflict? Suppose she's in her office closing a deal on the phone and a secretary on maternity leave comes in with her new baby. The lawyer tells the person on the phone she will have to call back. She holds the baby lovingly, and when the secretary departs, the lawyer sniffles and her eyes water. She reaches for the phone to make her call but hangs up because she needs more time to compose herself.

Main Trait: Does your character already have a dominant trait? Is he or she a bully, a victim, a gambler, a pedant, a snob, a social climber?

Humanizing Trait: This is what keeps the character from being too clichéd. For example, the bully apologizes but keeps right on bullying; the gambler is generous; the pedant has written several books that he cannot get published; the snob is secretly insecure; the social climber has lived with lifelong embarrassment over alcoholic parents.

Profession: The character's work might very well support the main trait. The bully could be a lawyer, or he could be the court stenographer who is meek in court and truculent at home where he cross-examines his family. The victim might answer letters of complaint for a company. The gambler could be a stockbroker; the pedant could be a librarian instead of a professor; the snob who arranges teenagers' dances, cruelly excluding some kids, could be director of admissions for a fancy school. The social climber could be a society reporter, making a living out of her obsession with wealth.

Address: The neighborhood, economic and social. Garbage-strewn streets, manicured lawns, or something in between. Inside the home, diapers strung in the kitchen tell us that a poor family lives there. Great art hung in the foyer indicates wealth and taste. Calendars displaying photos of nude women point to blue-collar bachelorhood. Your audience is reading the environment as they tune in the story.

Values: We are what we do, particularly in film, where external actions reveal inner states. Does your character spend time in yachts, health spas, bowling alleys, or soup kitchens serving the homeless? When he passes a needy person on the street, does he offer something? How does your character get around? In a dented old Dodge, a new Jaguar, a bus, on a skateboard? Does the character spend Saturday at the races or at an ashram?

Foil: Unlike the protagonist, the foil character does not change as a result of the film's action. Juxtaposing these characters enables the audience to measure growth in the protagonist. In *Working Girl*, two friends are both secretaries. One takes steps and risks to move up in the company, and the other does nothing. At the end, one is a wealthy executive, and the other is still a secretary, speaking and thinking the same as she did at the start of the film. At the beginning of the film both characters wear their hair the same way—teased and frosted—but the one who gets ahead changes her hairstyle after her boss suggests, "You might want to rethink your hair"; the new hairdo is a lot like the boss's.

Obsession: Obsessions are extremely gratifying to watch on the screen. Because they are usually portrayed visually and because they are predictable, the audience is able to anticipate what the character with the obsession will do. As a film starts, the audience has to concentrate to catch up to the characters. It has to tune in to the dialogue and make guesses as to what's going on and who's who. Later in the film, the audience knows that the obsession will prevail—even if the other characters do not. In *The Last Days of Hope and Time*, Albert Lee is addicted to basketball, shooting baskets night and day, years past the time when he should have grown up and become a breadwinner for his family. When his wife sets him up with a job interview, he agrees to go, but just when he is leaving the court he is lured back.

When I think of obsession in film, I think of Steve McQueen in *The Great Escape*. He keeps escaping from prison camp, getting caught by the Germans, being sent to solitary, bouncing his ball against the cell wall—over and over again. Or I think of David Warner, the defiant antagonist in *Morgan*, who is a rabid communist. We know this not from his speeches about economic justice but because of his obsession with the hammer and sickle, even to the point of planting flowers that bloom in a hammer-and-sickle pattern.

Goal: What the character wants should be very specific. A race car driver wants to win a specific race, perhaps because it is one his father lost. In *With Hands Up*, the boy's goal is freedom. In *Dog Day Afternoon*, the Al Pacino character wants money for his lover's sex-change operation.

Idol: Posters or portraits are the usual way of showing that the character is inspired by a legend. An ambitious coach might have a poster of Knute Rockne on his office wall. One of Mao Tse-tung or Madonna could indicate the character is a rebel. A poster of Marilyn Monroe could suggest that a character longs to be beautiful but lost. I can still see Jean-Paul Belmondo in *Breathless*, studying the poster of Humphrey Bogart and shaping his mouth to imitate Bogart's sneer.

Epitaph: Compressing a philosophy of life and a personality into a compact phrase is a way of bringing the character into sharper focus. The epitaph is how the character would like to be remembered. A well-meaning compulsive gambler might want the following phrase on his tombstone: "Two to one I'm in heaven." This is a man who does not see himself as harmful to others, but his wife and daughter may disagree. The daughter may feel cheated out of a college education and a catered wedding. Their lack of faith can be seen when he bursts into the house as they are eating dinner. He screams with excitement and throws $1,000 into the air, but the women keep on eating because they know he will lose this money soon. Perhaps the short is about how he revises his epitaph to read "Reformed Gambler."

Internal Conflicts: The inner child and the adult self may be at war. Let's use our gambler as an example again. The inner child wants to gamble, but the adult wants to support his family. We first see this character buying twenty lottery tickets from a newsstand. Later, when the inner adult is heeded, the character takes out a $20 bill and hesitantly asks for one ticket.

Interpersonal Conflicts: Such conflicts can add sparkle to a film and help drive the plot. Inspector Clouseau offends his police colleague, played by Herbert Lom, more than the thieves he pursues in the *Pink Panther* movies; if Groucho Marx did not defy Margaret Dumont in *Night at the Opera*, the movie wouldn't be nearly so funny; in *The Untouchables*, Eliot Ness would have less of a challenge without Al Capone as his quarry; and in *It's a Wonderful Life*, if not for Lionel Barrymore, Jimmy Stewart would have left for New York, forgotten his hometown, and left Donna Reed to marry someone else.

Societal and Environmental Conflicts: A character struggling against the severe climate of the Swiss Alps as he escapes over the border is clearly having a conflict with his environment. But the conflict need not be confined to the physical environment. In my own short *Happy Birthday to Me*, Linda is an actress who has tried to beat the long odds of succeeding in show business. But as she turns thirty, she gives herself one final day to get cast in a role before giving up acting for good. The various people who audition and reject Linda are the collective social obstacle: the catatonic off-broadway director; the ad agent who won't cast her but wants her home phone number.

Best Thing that Could Happen to This Character (which could turn out to be the worst): In *The Laureate*, a Russian émigré author works as a hotel porter until one day he receives a check from a publisher who wants to publish his latest novel. Immediately, he quits his job and looks forward to a successful life as a writer. When he meets the editor of the book, she talks about adding sex and sadism to the novel. He returns the check and takes a job as a babysitter.

Worst Thing that Could Happen to This Character (which could turn out to be the best): I draw from the screenplay in progress by my student Darryl McCaine. An upwardly mobile dentist has one child, a daughter whom he wants to go to dental school. After she gets accepted, she falls in love with a musician who shows little chance of commercial success and who gets her pregnant. The dentist is enraged. It is the worst thing that could happen to him. But the couple get married, and the dentist stifles his anger. At the end of the story, he has an adorable grandchild around the house, and when he opens his heart, he trains his son-in-law as a dental technician and reveals his own great love of jazz, buried long ago when he entered dental school. He comes to appreciate his son-in-law and plays jazz with him.

Why the Audience Will Root for This Character: Compared with psychological truth, film truth is narrower and simpler. Audiences are likely to root for attractive people pitted against surly-looking people. Even Konstantin

Stanislavsky, who invented modern acting and challenged stereo-typical casting, conceded this point. Audiences also root for people who can demonstrate mastery of some field; for victims of circumstance to master their fate; for antiheroes, whose goodness may be buried beneath a scowling surface. They also root for people who are funny, naive, well-meaning but inept. Jerry Lewis portrayed characters on the screen who exhibited all these traits.

Voice: Here the objective is to describe the inciting incident (which kicks off a sequence of events that changes the status quo). The description should incorporate the language the character uses—e.g., profane or professorial—and the viewpoint, which is the narrow focus of the character. It is important that the character does not have the writer's Olympian judgments. The character sees the world of the film from a narrow perspective.

Let's do a character profile of Linda, the actress in *Happy Birthday to Me.*

Sample Character Profile: Linda

Age: Today is her thirtieth birthday, a day of taking stock, a day of decision. She has one more day to harvest the efforts of her youth before saying good-bye to her dreams of success in show business.

Main Trait: She has a modest but not compelling talent, good looks, and good cheer but no star quality. She deceives herself with a head full of fantasies that tell her stardom is imminent.

Humanizing Trait: A capacity for honest self-assessment.

Profession: Actress. But is she? According to the timetable she established for herself, her early twenties were to be spent on preliminaries: taking acting classes, auditioning, getting an agent, following leads in the trade papers, working in summer stock. In her late twenties she wanted to get commercials to live on, off-Broadway parts to develop her art. In her thirties, she expected stardom. But success has eluded her. Her husband has moved to Chicago and wants to know whether she is joining him or ending the marriage.

Address: She lives in a seedy neighborhood in New York, in an apartment she never cleans, which has a bathtub in the kitchen and a floor littered with the trade papers of show business publications that feed her fantasies.

Values: Stanislavsky would say that she loves herself in art rather than the art in herself. She prizes the memory of her acting triumphs.

Foil: A self-deceived, pretentious director who fails to cast her in his poetic drama.

Obsession: To break her low batting average at finding acting jobs and get something worth staying in New York for.

Goal: To be an Academy Award–winning actress.

Idol: Claire Bloom, whom she resembles.

Epitaph: She Lit the Sky in Summer Stock.

Internal Conflicts: She doubts whether she has enough talent and staying power to be a working actor.

Interpersonal Conflicts: She and her husband will break up if she does not go to Chicago with him.

Societal and Environmental Conflicts: Her auditions cause her apathy or pain.

Best Thing That Could Happen to This Character (which could turn out to be the worst): She could get a part that sustains her illusions even if her husband leaves her.

Worst Thing That Could Happen to This Character (which could turn out to be the best): She cannot get the off-Broadway part she covets. She renews her marriage and has children.

Why the Audience Will Root for This Character: She is brave, gutsy, pretty, self-mocking, and not untalented.

Voice: The inciting incident is a telegram from her husband, who is coming to New York to settle once and for all whether their marriage will be terminated or renewed in Chicago. Her inner voice says: "Well, Linda. Happy birthday. Thirty years old and where are your little footprints in the sands of time? No husband anymore. No children. No Broadway stardom. Where are those headlines you were supposed to make?" She hears a minister delivering her funeral oration: "The early demise of Linda Brooks makes all our hearts heavy. The world, and especially the theater, seems dimmer without her radiant beauty. We remember especially her luminous portrayal of Elizabeth, the queen, at Roanoke High School. Others were privileged to see her off-Broadway debut in *Out, Brief Candle.*" The audience is beginning to root for Linda because her self-talk has irony and humor. Her inner monologues become a device in the film. They build a bond with the audience called empathy.

Creating Empathy

On the screen, we see an old man pushing a wheelbarrow up a hill. He doesn't get our attention until suddenly the wheelbarrow starts to go backward. He starts to go backward too. Our muscles tighten. We have an urge to get up from our seats to help him regain his footing. He starts out slower than before, but pretty soon he gets up to speed. He passes the point where he lost ground before. He almost reaches the top, then stops. He starts again, goes backward a step, and then gives it all he's got and makes it to the top. This man could be a mass murderer in the next scene, but right now we are bonded with him.

This is empathy, identification with a character that causes the audience to root for him or her. The empathy can build slowly as the character gradually responds to choices and obstacles. The audience will be more likely to root for a protagonist if he or she responds in an endearing way, is funny, charming, more skillful than most of them are, more appealing than his or her adversaries, undervalued by other characters, wrongly accused of or over-punished for a wrongdoing. Jean Valjean in *Les Miserables* is sentenced to a long prison sentence for stealing a loaf of bread to feed his sister's starving family. The Russian émigré writer in *The Laureate* is modest, shuns praise, makes the most of his circum-stances, is undervalued in his menial job. The hero of *Welcome to I.A.* is certainly undervalued when people in the same room with him cannot even see him at his own birthday party. All the skaters in *Skater Dater*, especially the lead, are extremely skillful. The protagonist gets our sympathy when he breaks ranks with the other boys in order to pursue a girl.

Dialects of the Film Language

As you write your film and begin to visualize it, you may be attracted to any number of technical choices to enhance your story. The normal camera speed is twenty-four frames per second in film and thirty frames per second in video. You can undercrank (shoot at eight, twelve, or sixteen frames per second), which speeds up the action in a comical way. To make action appear slow, graceful, and poetic, you can overcrank (shoot at forty-eight, sixty-four, or more frames per second), using a camera with a variable-speed motor. For even slower action, you can use a high-speed motor. You can do time-lapse photography wherein you shoot one frame every few hours for the purpose of showing a flower bloom or wither. In the lab, you can use fades, dissolves, superimpositions, and so forth. In video, you can use a paint box and do tricks with your image.

You can also shoot in black and white, which is used to evoke earlier decades of the twentieth century or to inform your audience to brace itself for a sober film. One such film is *That Burning Question*, a very serious look at relationships. You can scratch and dirty your negative to make it look like archival footage as in *With Hands Up*.

Opticals and effects are nice, but a good story is your best bet for reaching an audience. In chapters 4–8, we'll consider how to develop your story from a rough idea to a finished screenplay. This means starting with experiences you know to be true and expanding them in ways described in the next chapter.

4

Developing
the
Idea

EVERY SCREENPLAY HAS A PREMISE AND A PROTAGONIST. You can
start with a premise and then use the character form to design a
protagonist whose action will illustrate the premise. Or you can
start with a protagonist and then find ways to develop and test
this character, often by asking those questions on the form: what
are the best and worst things that can happen to him or her. The
answers should help you find a premise.

After you decide on a premise and a protagonist, you need to do
the following in order to develop your script. Create an antagonist, a character who opposes the protagonist with sufficient force
to threaten him or her and put the outcome in doubt; add other
characters as you need them. Develop plot and structure ideas
found through the step outline. Expand your story after using a
story checklist. Write the treatment; revise it after feedback.
Write a first draft with dialogue; convert dialogue to action.
Discover the controlling idea (what your screenplay is all about);
restructure; focus and unify the screenplay by asking yourself how

every scene supports the controlling idea. Unify your script and check your structure to make sure you have taken the audience on a good roller-coaster ride. And finally, hold a reading to get feedback; revise. After that, the dialogue refinement continues through rehearsals, shooting, and editing.

Learn from Early Dialogue

The above sequence is the ideal, but, in fact, the mind and imagination are wayward, like toddlers, running from one distraction to another with you in pursuit. You may be plotting your story and get dialogue ideas. Write them down, but remember that you want to *show*, not tell. The most honored shorts have little or no dialogue. Visual storytelling often comes after replacing dialogue with action. Committing to dialogue and polishing it before you know much about your hero and your screenplay will cost you time, and then you will be reluctant to throw the dialogue out if it no longer works. The most valuable thing about early dialogue is that you can comb through it for ideas, actions, and scenes. If two brothers are talking and one tells the other about saving his life when he was drowning, you may stumble into a rescue scene that will show in action, not words, how their relationship develops. More on conversion of dialogue to action later.

The Status Quo

Drama is sudden change under pressure from fast-breaking events. Your audience needs to know the point of departure, what the situation is before the action of the screenplay creates changes. Is your story about the class clown who contracts a mortal illness, loses his sense of humor, and then goes out laughing? You need to establish the clown before you tell the audience about the patient. If a daughter rebels after a lifetime of compliance, the audience needs to see the daughter conforming so that her later rebellion is gratifying.

The Foil

Unlike the protagonist, the foil does not change his or her values and is often a force to bring the protagonist back to the way things used to be. Suppose you want to write about the decline of a promising high school pitcher from a small town who goes away on a scholarship, meets a sexy townie on drugs, and self-destructs. His status quo is that he is a model son, has top grades, a girlfriend he has known since kindergarten, with whom he has a chaste relationship, and a great shutout record. When he changes later, his girlfriend does not. She retains her wholesome hometown values and becomes the foil when she goes to his college to try to reclaim him.

The Inciting Incident

The inciting incident upsets the status quo and causes the character to take an unaccustomed action. It has been said that many great stories begin with a journey, which takes the protagonist to new experiences, a new set of people, values, and issues. The character then makes choices that cause him or her to relinquish original values. This is also called *taking an action*. A female cop goes undercover. A runaway wife joins the circus. A truant officer runs off with a teenage singer.

The pitcher's journey begins when he says good-bye to his

parents and girlfriend at the bus station and heads for the college town where he meets the pivotal character, the femme fatale who awakens appetites he has suppressed. Meeting her and feeling hopelessly attracted to her is the inciting incident. She uses drugs, gets him to buy a motorcycle with his housing and food money, dares him to do dangerous bike stunts with her, and embroils him in a triangle when her violent boyfriend gets out of jail. Just before the pitcher gets into a violent fight with the biker, which will lead to his self-destruction, his hometown girlfriend comes to visit him. She pleads with him to give up the other woman, the violence she attracts, and the drugs she uses.

The inciting incident need not be a person. It can be a storm, a car's or plane's engine trouble, the outbreak of war. It can be a sudden quarrel, robbery, or murder. On TV sitcoms, the inciting incident is frequently the visiting relative or the old war buddy who shows up with a different set of values and tests the status quo values of the principals. In *Hamlet*, the death of the prince's father is the inciting incident which brings Hamlet home to explore foul play. In *Hamaki*, the destabilizing event for a twelve-year-old girl of mixed ancestry is the arrival of her Korean grandmother, who upsets the girl's expectations.

Raise the Stakes

This term, of course, comes from poker. It is what the character has at risk, stands to lose. In most stories, the stakes go up at least twice. In *The Bet*, a short directed by Ted Demme, a compulsive gambler is late with his payment on a wager he has lost. At first he is warned verbally. Then the stakes get raised when a collector breaks his thumb as a stronger message to pay up. When he still does not pay, the mob wants a share in the deli business he owns with his upright brother. An uncle gives him a tip that pays off; he wins enough money on the bet to cover the debt and more. But then, on the way out, he overhears a tout talking about another sure thing. Instead of paying the mob, he goes back to the betting window for one more score.

Plotting Takes Patience

Plotting can be a slow process. My own mentor, Thornton Wilder—whom I met when he became a daily visitor to rehearsals of his play *Skin of Our Teeth*, which I was then directing at Harvard—used to find plotting exhausting. He could do it for only an hour at a time. Yet his play *The Merchant of Yonkers* was an intricate farce rewritten in his later years. The idea started out as a play by the German Johann Nepomuk Nestroy. Wilder's version flopped on Broadway, was revived successfully, and later was made into a movie. Then it was adapted for the musical stage and became the long-running hit *Hello, Dolly!* So patient plotting can pay off. Developing the plot requires you to make your protagonist pay an increasingly greater price for his or her initial choice.

Creating a Step Outline

Many professional screenwriters prepare a step outline to develop their plot. Here's how to create one. Get a set of three-by-five-inch index cards that you can put on a table or bulletin board and move around. Each card will represent a specific scene in your story. It helps to number the cards, but use a pencil because you will be reshuffling the order of scenes and will have to do some erasing. You can also do a step outline on a computer, but the cards work better because your fingers make tactile contact with your story.

You will be writing the actions, the building blocks of your plot, in caps. Use *action verbs* that lead to change. So don't write, "He ENTERS room, LIGHTS lamp," but rather, "He BREAKS INTO room, FINDS crack." "Boy FISHES" is not going to get your story very far unless it is followed by "PULLS UP dead body." That will jump-start your story.

Finding Structure   After you have filled out twenty to thirty cards, study them and try to see the *structural arc* of your story. Have you found the best order of scenes so that you are introducing *progressive complications* and increasing *jeopardy*, causing the audience to worry about the protagonist? These two elements help build tension. The other part of structure is *orchestration of the plot*—the rising and falling of tension. In a well-orchestrated story, a tense and serious scene is followed by a funny scene, a fast scene by a slow one. A rise in tension is often followed by a plateau where you can let the audience rest, lulling them into a false sense of security as the action *appears* to de-escalate. During a plateau moment when the tension cools, a man and woman running from the bad guys feel safe enough to explore their own relationship. But in many films, when they start to make love, their pursuers resurface to keep the tension unresolved. Usually, a man and woman do not complete the act of lovemaking until the antagonist has been vanquished.

A plateau scene could also be a comic montage with music. Or it could be a subplot scene. In *Time Expired*, mentioned earlier, the main action is the triangle between Bobby, his wife, and his transvestite lover. The comic subplot is about Bobby's mother, who obsesses over the shepherd's pie she wants to cook for him and the new clothes she wants to buy him. Another subplot involves the brother, who is obsessed with comic books and would never notice anything amiss. We are amused at the irrelevance of these issues to a man trying to decide whether he belongs to his wife or his transvestite lover.

While looking for structure, do not overlook the obvious. Do you have a first, second, and third act—a beginning, middle, and end? Even if the rules for shorts are somewhat relaxed, your audience must have rising expectations.

Sample Step Outline: Jonathan's Story

The following step outline is an expansion of the anecdote about my son Jonathan's and my trip to Washington, which I recounted in chapter 3. The premise is that a shy child blossoms rapidly when the right circumstances permit him to flower. A psychologist told me a few years later that Jonathan was perfectly normal. He was just, in her words, "Slow to warm up." The acceleration of such slowness could be gratifying on film. Watch out for the sudden twist of plot. I have advanced the children's ages because older child actors are easier to work with.

1. Brothers Danny and Jonathan (J.), ages five and seven, QUARREL over blocks.
2. Boys RACE to intercom to greet divorced father (F.), calling from lobby. Danny WINS.
3. F. SWOOPS them up at downstairs elevator. OFF TO PARTY.
4. At party J. MEETS Aunt Linda and Cousin Peter. Peter is different; he shares.
5. A mime ENTERTAINS, IMITATES loud, aggressive Danny.
6. Two cousins bond. Linda INVITES J. to D.C.

7. F. BUYS sons ridable toy car and WATCHES. TELLS them to share.

8. J. FIGHTS with brother over car. PHONES F. to arrange promised trip to D.C.˜

9. F. PHONES Linda with flight info. (landing D.C. 9:00 A.M.). She will watch J. while he goes to Senate, then White House.

10. F. PICKS UP J. Danny DEMANDS F. FIX broken car, which makes him LOSE briefing paper for senator.

11. On plane they LEARN of flight delay.

12. Stewardess ANNOUNCES further delay. Finally, flight CANCELED.

13. Linda WAITS at gate with Peter. ANNOUNCEMENT. Linda DRIVES OFF. Peter LOOKS OUT window, forlorn.

14. J. and F.'s plane TAKES OFF.

15. They ARRIVE D.C. No Linda. F. PHONES Linda. No answer. J. watches closely.

16. F. and J. TAKE cab. J. STUDIES watch, ASKS how long to Capitol. Talkative cabbie EXPLAINS four sections of D.C. zones.

17. Senate. Projectionist STARTS film in darkened committee room. Film RIPS.

18. In cab, F. TENSELY WARNS J. to be on good behavior with senators.

19. Senate. Projector RESTARTED. Film RIPS AGAIN. Lights GO ON.

20. J. and F.'s cab ARRIVES Senate Bldg. F. TRIES TO HURRY J., who says "Carry me." "Why?" "I'm afraid the men won't like me." F.: "You're too old to be carried. I refuse."

21. F. CLIMBS steps with J. in arms.

22. F. and J. RUSH to near-empty room, SEE woman who

appeared in film, named Maria Guzman. F. breathless but
WHISPERS greeting. They HUG. He ASKS HER TO
WATCH J. She PROTESTS that this is her first day in
Washington. "Just take him to your hotel." She gives him
hotel name, goes back to watching herself on screen. F.
HANDS her money, but she's watching herself on screen and
DROPS money. J. PICKS it up.

23. J. CHASES cab outside Senate.
24. ARRIVE hotel. Maria Guzman doubts fare, but J. says they
have gone through three zones, adds tip.
25. J. CALLS Linda, who says come over.

Entering the Slipstream: We interrupt this step outline for a very important message on writing. I was getting bored.
Were you? This is a useful feeling when writing. It means you
have to restimulate interest by injecting a new idea into the
process. Otherwise the film is headed toward dullsville. It is
helpful to put into words precisely what is wrong with your
script. It is like sending specifications to your unconscious on
what you are looking for. The step I needed was a cinematic event
that would match the inner growth of Jonathan on this trip. At
this very point in the step outline, I slid into the *cinematic slipstream*. This is a state where your rate of creativity is suddenly
enhanced, where ideas drift in unbidden, where epiphanies dance
onto your screen or page.

My new idea was to create a growth step for Jonathan by having
an unreliable adult at the wheel of the cab, perhaps an alcoholic, so
he would have to save the day by taking over the steering wheel.
This step would enhance his low self-esteem. When he feels better
about himself, we feel better. It took me just a few minutes to

refine the idea and integrate it into the plot and the character of Jonathan, who fears that he cannot come through for his father. After only a little more time, I was able to pin down the driver's problem. He would be diabetic rather than an alcoholic (for the sake of simplicity and logic) and would fall into a diabetic coma. A friend of mine, Dr. David Singer, a specialist in diabetes, later advised me on how the coma could happen—by consuming alcohol on an empty stomach.

The term *slipstream* originated in the field of aviation to describe the phenomenon whereby a plane gets a sudden burst of velocity by riding winds that propel it forward. In the cinematic slipstream, you may experience a natural high when creativity speeds up. Do not assume you can ignore this rush and get it back. Turn off your phone, close your door, and act as if under a spell that will not last forever. Write as fast as you can, to get the full benefit of this surge of creativity. Do not worry about form or grammar, just keep generating ideas.

And now back to the step outline.

26. In cab, J. SEES driver grow sleepy. Driver's eyes swim. He SLUMPS backward, STEERS wrong way downhill on a one-way street. J. SHAKES him and then JUMPS into front seat. Driver STEERS cab from parked cars, CLOSES eyes as he goes through red traffic signal, siren screaming after them. Finally, he comes to clogged intersection, HEADS BROADSIDE into traffic. J. SLIDES DOWN in seat, BRAKES, then SLAMS shift lever into park as police CATCH UP.
27. Linda's house. Police car PULLS UP with J. Cop talks to Linda as J. and Peter CHASE each other into the backyard.
28. F. ARRIVES, TRIES to hug J., but J. still CHASING Peter. F. watches a new J. who is bold, not shy.

29. N.Y. F. DROPS OFF J. in front of house where brother
Danny is riding toy car. Danny tells J. he can't have a turn,
but J. doesn't care. He SHOWS police badge from D.C. cops
and PULLS OVER Danny for a traffic stop. Danny COVETS
the badge, even offers the car in exchange for it, but J.
REFUSES. F. SCOOPS up Danny, then goes to hug J. good-
bye, but J. extends hand, shakes with F. Finally, GIVES him
a big hug with mother watching.

The emergency driving in step 25 gives Jonathan instant adult
status. It also allows for cinematic thrills and near misses for the
audience. In later chapters, you will see for yourself how the story
is developed further.

5

Developing
the
Treatment

IT HAS BEEN SAID that the best thing about film is that it is in the present tense. It is also the biggest disadvantage. Developing the forward momentum of your film begins with the *treatment*. A treatment is a prose description, written in the present tense, of what the audience will see on the screen. It resembles a short story, but the emphasis is on action *now*. Dialogue is summarized and is rarely spelled out. You should concentrate on external action. Don't linger over descriptions of the sky and the sunset, which may or may not be filmable on the day you have your cast and crew ready, depending on light and weather conditions. The most crucial part of the writing is the choice of verbs, because you are describing actions that the characters take, and action is usually cinematic.

At this stage, your mind is still the toddler, running here and there, controlled by whim. Later the parent will impose discipline on the ideas, make them logical and connected. Even though your cards have numbers (with erasures), stay open to new ideas, which may arrive in a very tentative and wistful way. Often good ideas do not bang on the door of your consciousness. At first you may feel that your mind is wandering. But entertain these visitors to your creative process. An idea could arrive in disguise, dressed as a whole new idea for another screenplay. Just take notes and examine the idea for its relevance to the script you are doing at the moment.

This is a very creative stage in the writing process. Feel free to add scenes, change locations, and so forth. Before the clay hardens, you can let your mind play spontaneously. Therefore don't be too judgmental of your own writing. Don't stop to correct your grammar, spelling, or story inconsistencies. It's more important to get it written than to get it right. This is a good time to learn from your spontaneous writing, to find out what you unconsciously think. In fact, you should be courting your unconscious at this stage of the writing. Let characters arrive and depart. Study them to see what they offer before you clean up the cast list and combine characters.

Remember to look for a visual approach to every scene. (It's always better to show the action rather than describe it in dialogue.) But don't get stuck. If you can't think of a visual approach right away, keep moving and give yourself an IOU. When I write, I really pile up the IOUs. I record them on a separate list and come back to them later.

This is a good time to think about which physical locations would best serve the plot and the characters. If someone is trying to save another from suicide, don't set the scene in a café. Set it on a ledge. If a character's personality is formed by a social background, find ways of putting him or her in environments that project that background and those values.

A treatment for a short does not amount to many pages of text. Seven to ten pages roughly equal a half hour of film time. After you have written a rough draft revise it as necessary but don't invest an inordinate amount of time in the effort. You may very well have to make more revisions after getting feedback from others. Note that this is the time for supportive reactions from friends, whose criticism will be gentle. Later, you can subject your screenplay to tougher scrutiny. Never give the original of your finished treatment to a teacher or a friend or to anyone else. Keep it and make copies, or it is liable to get lost.

To help you develop a treatment for your story, I'll be asking you a series of questions in this chapter. These questions are meant to serve as a checklist for determining whether your story has all the necessary ingredients. (I have already introduced, in chapter 4, a number of these ingredients: protagonist, antagonist, status quo, foil, inciting incident, and raising the stakes.) Do not get stalled if you cannot answer a given question. Move on to the next one. And don't worry if certain questions do not apply to your story. You are not taking a Graduate Record Exam but simply considering some questions to stimulate the creative process. If this exercise tells you that your script is missing an ingredient but you cannot immediately supply it, make a note to yourself for future reference. It's a good idea to go through the list of questions a few times, revising the story and characters here and there, like a painter who might create a portrait by moving the brush from the face to the feet to the arm.

Does Your Story Have a Hook?

A hook compels an audience to abandon other preoccupations and focus on your film. Think of it this way. Your film has won festival prizes and you have schemed to get an executive in Hollywood to watch it. He inserts the tape in his VCR and hits the "play" button. During your crucial boy-meets-girl scene, the phone rings and he answers it. Will he tell the caller he'll phone back later so he can continue watching the tape? Or stop the tape and have a phone conversation? Or talk while the tape runs? Maybe the hook is so strong that he'll go back and play the tape from the beginning and tell his secretary to hold his calls.

Here is an example of a good hook. A girl and her dog witness a murder. The killer chases them and kills the girl, but the dog escapes. The hook compels the audience to root for the dog to lead the authorities to the murdered girl and the killer. The hook is not always baited with hard-core, life-and-death action, but the audience should bond with the protagonist right away. Bonding means that the audience wants for the hero what he wants for himself—a promotion at work, an apology, vengeance against a bully, and so forth.

The hook may be a situation rather than a character. Perhaps the hook is a mystery that the audience cannot second-guess and so will stick around to watch the resolution. Or maybe there is something a little off about the opening scenes that makes the audience curious. A husband and wife enjoy the toasts of friends gathered for their anniversary dinner. They retire wordlessly, each to one side of the bed, and the man reaches for a hidden gun.

What Is Your Point of Attack?

The writer thinks of his or her characters as having a history that explains why they behave as they do. But telling the whole story makes the script less dramatic and takes up valuable screen time. The point of attack is the place where the story starts on the screen. The film will be more watchable if you begin with the action and explain the background (back story) later. Often students write a long buildup to the action with flashbacks in the beginning of the script. If you're tempted to do this, ask yourself whether you can start your story later, when the action starts. (See "Do You Need a Back Story?" later in this chapter and the discussion of back story in chapter 6.)

When he wrote *Hamlet*, Shakespeare did not begin his story at Wittenburg University, where the prince hears the news of his father's death. Instead, he began with the action of the ghost arriving in the mist to alert Hamlet about foul play.

Take another example from the film *Proof*, where the action starts right after titles. A car full of good old boys are teasing a more reticent "friend" about *proving* that he is not a coward, referring to a past incident in which he failed a test of courage. Offering him a second chance, they drive him to the Pecos Parachute School. They carry him out of the car and send him up in a rickety plane, not realizing that the owner's wife, who is a little daft, has switched her laundry with his parachute. When they discover their error, the friends take the remaining laundry and lay it on the ground, spelling out the message "Don't jump."

The writer-director, Kevin Reynolds, could have started this film in the past with the incident that showed the man's cowardice, but instead it starts three minutes before the plane takes off.

Does Your Story Have Rising Action?

Earlier I mentioned rising action, increasing stakes, or, to use another term common in screenwriting, progressive complications, which push the protagonists away from the normal and conventional. Things must get worse before they can get better— if they ever do. In a full-length screenplay, there are plot points, according to the Syd Field, where the story line veers in a different direction, also raising the stakes. In a short, where the rules are looser, you may not need more than one plot point.

My favorite rising-action film is *The Swiss Family Robinson*, in which a family is shipwrecked and then continually survives attacks from tigers, natives, and all manner of perils. These are sequential complications. Where there are progressive complications, the sense of jeopardy keeps on intensifying. An example: Your main character has an altercation with a truck driver after their vehicles almost collide. Each threatens the other, but finally the hero drives off. In stage 2, the truck driver sees this man again and tries to scrape his car, then chases him. In stage 3, the truck driver chases him on foot with a tire iron. He strikes him once on the shoulder, then keels over, winded from the chase. In stage 4, the truck driver gets a heart attack from running.

Aisle Six is a very original short in which high school norms are reversed so that girls ignore football players and develop crushes on boys studying plumbing, which is a prestigious career. One of the students gets a notion to be different. He announces at dinner to his girlfriend and her family that he wants to go to MIT and become an electrical engineer. It puts a pall over the occasion. The rising action progressively pits him against society until he self-destructs. The film very effectively parodies a conformist society in which the one who dares to be different perishes from lack of support.

How do you go about raising the stakes? When you are elaborating your action in the step outline, ask what is the logical extreme of your character's action. Drama is not about the ordinary or the expected. It is about the unusual. In my first version of the step outline of the short about my son Jonathan, he simply took a cab without incident from Maria Guzman's hotel to Linda's house, and the camera froze on his more confident expression. But I kept doubting whether the action really kept rising after he mastered the taxi rules.

Then I remembered a short I had once made with my sons. It was directed and photographed by the real Jonathan, who was by then, at age eight, a very demanding director. It was about a kidnapped boy who escaped by driving a car. Since so many children fantasize about driving a car, I wondered whether there was a way to integrate into the story a scene with a kid driving a car in traffic. Then I applied my *rule of three* whereby things get: (1) somewhat worse, then (2) a lot worse, and finally (3) as bad as they can get! As soon as one problem is solved, another arises.

Is There an "Or Else"?

This is the threat that the antagonist makes to the protagonist. It evokes what will happen if the protagonist fails to give the antagonist what he wants. It also raises the stakes that the protagonist stands to lose. Your "or else" should be shown visually and should be concrete, not vague. My favorite "or else" scene occurs in *The Gambler*, written by James Toback. Burt Young as a Mafia-style collector comes to get money from a literature professor, played by James Caan, who has gambled on his college's team. After talking about books and a family member who actually reads, Burt Young seems ready to leave without the money. Just before he heads for the door, he pushes over a standing bookcase, sending its contents flying. It is a graphic way of saying that if he does not get the money, brute force will topple the professor's world.

Are You Showing, Not Telling?

I have discussed this question earlier, but it is one that you will keep asking yourself for as long as you are writing screenplays or making films. Your goal is to tell the story through action and pictures, rather than through dialogue. Don't have characters say they're going to attack the castle. Show the attack. It is permissible to announce what the characters are going to do *only if everything is to go wrong*. (See the discussion of logistical dialogue in chapter 6.) Then you spell out in dialogue the plan that later goes awry.

You may ask, What's wrong with telling through dialogue? It deprives the audience of their main activity: *guessing*, figuring out what happened before the action takes place as well as what the protagonist will do when barriers appear. It deprives them of guessing the real thoughts of the characters, their true intentions. It would be gilding the lily if I put Jonathan's sibling rivalry problems into words in the script. The feelings have to be *shown*. In real life, a sensitive psychiatrist can monitor incremental changes in self-assertiveness, but in a film, changes play better in the language of action.

Is the Protagonist Under
Time Pressure?

Having shown the "or else," have you put time pressure on your hero, making him or her race against a deadline to save the situation? In *The Dog Ate It*, a sadistic professor taunts a student playboy, who then stays up all night to finish a paper due the next morning. After a catnap, the hero wakes to see his dog chewing some typed pages to bits. He goes to class empty-handed. But wait—the dog has in fact *not* chewed the real paper. Sensing that he caused a problem, the dog grabs it like a newspaper and races to class just as the professor is unleashing his scorn on the student. The filmmaker intercuts between the professor and the dog racing to class.

High Noon contains a classic example of time pressure. At noon, the sheriff (Gary Cooper) must face the town's villain and possibly kill him, despite the entreaties of his nonviolent Quaker wife (Grace Kelly). The villain is to arrive by train at the stroke of noon. In all key scenes, a clock shows that the deadline is coming up.

Is There a Pivotal Character?

This person is the instrument of change. Through the actions of the pivotal character, the protagonist is prompted to change the status quo by taking action. In *Marilyn Hotchkiss's Ballroom Dancing and Charm School*, the status quo is the rough way boys behave toward girls, illustrated by one young lady's black eye from a coed game of British Bulldog. The pivotal character, Mrs. Hotchkiss, a humorless, droning teacher committed to dancing and good manners, encourages the boys to pivot from their childhood antipathy toward girls into a world of civility between the sexes.

In *That Burning Question*, a couple who cannot seem to commit to each other are on the subway. The man, a journalist, is going to cover the story of a man who has threatened to set himself afire if his woman does not take him back. When she finally does, the couple realize what is missing in their own relationship. The pivotal character is the man prepared to incinerate himself for love.

Does Your Story Have Unity?

Does every scene contribute to the story, and does the story come full circle to clarify changes? Often the short begins and ends in the same location, emphasizing the change that has taken place in the course of the story. After the experience of the story, the protagonist should be changed. *That Burning Question* begins and ends with the couple on the subway, talking about their noncommittal relationship. As they ride back, they are sobered, thoughtful, unable to continue a relationship without commitment.

Sandino Bambino starts as the idealistic but mushy-headed Martin applies for a job with a supermarket, telling the cynical bosses that he believes supermarkets have a great future. While Martin worries about international injustice, his girlfriend runs off with his father. The film ends with Martin working as a clown, passing out handbills in front of the same supermarket. His idealism and naïveté have soured into disillusionment.

Do You Need a Back Story?

The back story explains those events in the past that caused the protagonist or antagonist to behave in a certain way. For example, a mean person confesses he is a survivor of child abuse. You need to include a back story only when the present story needs justification. The back story can take the form of a flashback or a dialogue retelling. The disadvantage of a flashback is that if the character recalls his or her childhood, you lose momentum while the audience transfers its sympathy from the adult actor to the child actor (as in *The Prince of Tides*). It sometimes helps to have the voice of the actor playing the mature character narrate the past experience. Such scenes should be held to a minimum because while the back story is filled in, the emotional buildup is on hold. You want to keep the film visual. But if explanations are important, dialogue may be the only way. More on this in the next chapter.

Does Your Character Have a Strong Goal?

The simpler the goal, the more focused, the easier it is for the audience to side with the character in all of his or her adventures. In *E.T.*, the alien's goal is simply to go home. In *Fugu*, the character's goal is to break the bonds of his narrow life as an actuary. In a Japanese restaurant, he meets a woman who will share "fugu," a fish with aphrodisiac properties. In *Welcome to I.A.*, Paul finds himself invisible at his own birthday party. His goal is to become visible again. The stronger, the more fundamental the goal, the stronger the film.

Does Your Character Take Charge?

In life there may be no correlation between effort and result, but not in drama or the film, long or short. *Character is destiny* is the unchanging rule. Make sure your character is challenged to solve his or her own problem. Even if the character is a psychiatric patient, the doctor may be an enabler but the protagonist has to work through the problem outside the office.

The steps your protagonist takes may be small ones, but pretty soon larger and larger actions and reactions are crashing around him or her. Take one of the biggest stories of our time: Gorbachev tries to humanize the Soviet system. The first step was *glasnost*, or openness and candor. Events kept changing until finally he was brought down by his own hang-up—belief in the communist system. His character finally did him in. People are often the battleground between two warring ideas, only one of which can survive.

Does Your Protagonist Change?

Is your leading character different at the end of the film? Drama is about character growth and change in a measurable, external way. Paul goes from invisible to visible in *Welcome to I.A.* In my step outline, Jonathan changes from a shy and diffident child to a bold and self-confident youngster. It is very human for the character to resist his or her own change—for a brave character to get scared under fire. I think of Roberto Rossellini's *General Della Rovere*, in which Vittorio De Sica plays a coward dressed as a general. People treat him with reverence, so he begins to behave heroically.

Is There a Strong POV on the World of the Story?

No two people will see this world with the same point of view (POV). What is *yours*? Consider, for example, the world of the army. To one person, the army is an arbitrary, antihuman organization with power-mad, sadistic leadership—a cheerless last refuge of righteous scoundrels. To another person, the army is a second chance for losers in the big world to redeem themselves. Another sees it as harsh on the outside but compassionate on the inside. Another claims that the standards of the army prepare you for survival during peace as well as war. Many people find a rare camaraderie in the army that you could never find in civilian life. Goldie Hawn's character in *Private Benjamin* starts out as a Jewish princess, but eventually she chooses army life over her former life of dependency and luxury.

Or take the world of advertising. One person can see this field as dominated by the tyranny of the client—a limited, overly cautious person with no taste. Another person might find the creative teamwork inspiring: the team who worked with Tom Hanks's character in *Nothing in Common* created an airline TV commercial that was really a warm, musical poem.

Locations should support your view of the worlds you are portraying. Think of the movie *Arthur*, where the manorial world and uniformed butler of Dudley Moore's Arthur are contrasted with the unkempt kitchen of Liza Minelli's working-class waitress, where her father sits in his undershirt.

Locations are more important in a short than in a sitcom episode, which is confined to a three-sided set for the most part. The short should take place in evocative environments that are interesting on their own—a pocket park, a lawn-bowling court, a botanical garden. I can think of several New York locales that are underrepresented in film, including Wave Hill, a mansion on the Hudson River with spectacular gardens; the castle or the zoo in Central Park; and the flower district, a distribution center for a million flowers a day.

What's in This Story for the Audience?

Charles Dickens said about his audience: "Make them laugh, make them cry, make them . . . wait." Now is the time to start thinking about your audience and how to reach them. In the beginning of the screenplay, you should be courting the audience and building trust. Reassure them that they are in good hands, that you will entertain them with comedy, drama, or suspense. Shorts work best if they have comedy in them—the kind of real, human, nonverbal comedy that audiences cannot get in a sitcom.

Do You Have a False Resolution?

This is the moment when the story *seems* to come to a logical conclusion. Sometimes the false resolution is unsatisfying, but since we are all accustomed to settling for less than we think we deserve, we accept this half a loaf. When the real resolution comes, it leaves us much more satisfied because we were first denied what we wanted. In *The Red Balloon*, we are sad when the bullies deflate the boy's balloon companion, and we think this is the final down ending. But suddenly from all parts of Paris, balloons swoop down and carry the boy off into the sky. This false resolution increases empathy when the boy is rewarded by the grateful community of balloons.

Sometimes, the opposite is true. The false resolution is satisfying, and the real resolution deliberately shocking. In *Night Movie*, the Arab teenager who learns to trust his Israeli captor is released to go home. It is the ending everybody is rooting for, but suddenly he turns a corner and runs into an Israeli jeep. He panics, runs, and is shot. Our shock is intensified, but this is exactly what the director, Gur Heller, wanted. Captor and prisoner have become buddies, but on the street he is a fleeing Arab who must have done something wrong.

Is the Ending a Mind-Sticker?

The ending is what people take away from a film. Shorts, in particular, should try for an ending that combines the surprising and the credible. In *The Lunch Date*, a woman goes into a cafeteria while waiting for a train. She puts her coat and packages down, gets herself a salad, puts it on a table, goes to the ladies' room, and comes back to find a homeless man eating her salad. She gets another fork, sits down, and, without exchanging a word, insists on sharing the salad. Later, he buys her a cup of coffee. As she goes to catch her train, she suddenly remembers her packages. She returns to the cafeteria, finds her packages *and* her salad untouched, at another table. The ending forces you to reexperience the film. She thought she was being generous to a homeless man, but it turns out *he* was generous to *her*. Professor Carrol Bardosh of New York University says that a misunderstanding, such as this one, is a frequent basis for a short film.

Endings are often character reversals. The drinker junks his collection of bottles. The decadent rebel in *Greasey Lake* sobers up after confronting death. The boy in *Skater Dater* gives up group values to date a girl. In *The Room*, a boy held prisoner by his father makes a fantasy escape. In *The Chaparral Prince*, a kitchen slave becomes liberated; in *Night Movie*, a captor becomes a friend.

Do You Have a Controlling Idea?

The premise is explicit, but the controlling idea is implicit, elusive rather than obvious. The controlling idea is the truth you want to communicate—in actions, not words. If you state the idea in words, it becomes propaganda. Jeff Sweet says in his book *The Dramatist's Toolkit* that if you as a writer want an audience to know something, do not have the character say two plus three equal five. You should say two plus X equal five. In other words, start your audience thinking and putting things together. They will enjoy the piece better as active observers of the story, rather than as students who are spoon-fed information.

The short *Walking the Dog* is a good example. It is the story of Etta, a woman of retirement age who runs an antiques store. Though she is unable to pay the rent, she cannot bear to sell anything in her store. All the objects are meaningful to her, particularly some yo-yos that belonged to her teenage son who died after winning a yo-yo championship. Joey, a budding juvenile delinquent, comes to rob her, but she sees something in him that reminds her of her dead son. Instead of calling the police, she tells him a little about the yo-yo and demonstrates the trick "walking the dog." She offers to give him a yo-yo if he will do an errand for her. In several fantasy scenes, the boy goes back to his bad habits, but eventually he gives up some of his antisocial ways. Etta stops clinging to the past and is able to part with her antiques in order to pay the rent. You could call the controlling idea in this film: "There is a time to give up what nourished you in the past but no longer does." If this message had been put into words, it would be resented by the viewer, who would say, "Entertain me but don't preach to me."

Sample Treatment: *Jonathan's Turn*

Here is the treatment I wrote about the story of Jonathan's experiences during our trip to Washington, D.C. I gave the treatment a title—"Jonathan's Turn"—which I later used for the screenplay and the finished film. Note the use of caps with directions for camera, sound effects (sometimes called FX), and music. Caps are also used with major characters on first appearance; initial capital letters are employed thereafter. All minor characters are identified here not by name but by profession (e.g., the Technicians, the Bartender) or relationship to another character (the Friend of the Chauffeur)—note the initial caps.

Jonathan's Turn

CAMERA IS AT THE EYE LEVEL OF A CHILD as JONATHAN, 6, a serious-looking child, is seen through the blocks he is building. His brother DANNY, 5, plays nearby. Danny looks over jealously and finally tries to "help." Jonathan protests, and soon the blocks have fallen. The MOTHER comes in to stop the screaming and crying. She asks Jonathan to let Danny have a turn. Jonathan storms out, furious.

The apartment intercom RINGS, and Danny stands on a chair to answer it. He listens a moment, hangs up, and screams, "Daddy's here!" As the boys leave, the Mother asks Jonathan not to be so grumpy. Inside the elevator, Danny calls the still-smarting Jonathan "Grumpy" and other names. The elevator door opens, and the LOW, WIDE-ANGLE CAMERA LOOKS UP to see the tall MIKE, 35, waiting for them. Jonathan leaps up, and Mike lifts him so he can TINKLE the lobby chandelier. Immediately, Danny starts to cry and will not shut up until Mike puts down Jonathan and lifts Danny, who swings the chandelier wildly back and forth as the Doorman winces and Mike rapidly moves off. Outside he gives each boy a watch. Danny puts his on with the numbers upside down, and Jonathan puts his on correctly. In the distance, we hear PARADE MUSIC.

We cut to the Macy's Thanksgiving Day Parade. Leggy marching girls. Bands. Floats. Giant balloons. Mike arrives with the boys. The children see a wall of adult bodies, a band moving past elbows and legs. Mike lifts Jonathan onto his shoulder for a better view. Immediately, Danny begins to wail. People standing around them roll their eyes and move away. Finally, Mike puts down Jonathan and puts Danny on his shoulders. Immediately, Danny's tears change to a grin. He eyes Jonathan, looking downcast, sticks out his tongue, and calls him "Sad Sack."

All three arrive at a Thanksgiving gathering. Adult legs wander around. Bodies separate; a child Danny's age throws him a ball, and the two begin to play. CAMERA MOVES to Jonathan looking lost. Mike takes his hand and takes him over to cousin LINDA with her son, PETER, 5. The bodies are kissing above them as Peter and Jonathan look at each other. Mike introduces them. Jonathan is paralyzed with shyness. As they awkwardly talk—Jonathan shows off his new watch—Linda and Mike make plans to see each other the next time he goes to Washington, D.C. Mike bends down as Jonathan whispers a question, asking what a cousin is. Mike replies that he's like a brother you don't have to live with. A smile curls around Jonathan's face as Linda puts a pilgrim hat on his head. CAMERA MOVES to Danny, wearing a turkey costume, charging at adults.

In their apartment, many days later, Danny looks at his watch, whose crystal is shattered. He grabs at Jonathan's but cannot remove it. Danny screams until the Mother comes in, carrying a cooking spoon, and lends Danny her own watch. Jonathan, smoldering, goes to the phone and calls his father. Reached at the office, Mike answers Jonathan's question about when they are going to see Peter. Mike says he is going to Washington next week. Linda is seen on the phone saying that she will pick up Jonathan at the airport and take him for the whole day; Peter plays in the background.

Mike buys their tickets at the airport. Clock in background reads 8:45. Settling into their seats on the plane, Mike uses Jonathan's watch to show his son the time when the plane will take off. Jonathan asks when Mike has to see the Senator (11:00) and when he has to be at the White House (12:00) and when he will be through (2:00). Inside the cockpit, some Technicians arrive and open up their tool kits. They open up a panel, and we see a Stewardess announce a slight delay on the flight. When we cut to an exterior shot of the plane, more Technicians are carrying their kits and climbing the stairs. We cut back to Mike and Jonathan, whose watch reads 9:35. He shows it to Mike, who gets worried.

In Washington, Jonathan and Mike exit the airport, still looking for Linda and Peter. They are not to be found. Other people wave and find each other. Mike leans down and warns Jonathan: he is taking him to the meeting with the Senator but does not want any "babyish" behavior. As a cab departs, we can hear Mike in a voice over (VO) warning that they are going to be with men who pass the laws and who do not like children to talk or act badly when they are meeting.

Inside the cab, Jonathan's thumb goes into his mouth as he leans against Mike, who takes it out. They both get out of the car at the congressional building. CAMERA TILTS UP to the intimidating enormity of the building. Mike starts to run up the stairs and looks back to Jonathan who has not moved. Mike goes back down, and Jonathan asks to be carried. He's afraid the men won't like him.

We cut to the inside of the building, where Mike, carrying Jonathan and breathing heavily, finally arrives at the top of the stairs and heads for the committee room, just as it empties out. People hurry past them, but a Senator sees Mike and asks him if his plane was late. Mike cannot catch his breath, but Jonathan gives the exact number of minutes they were delayed.

The Senator decides to reschedule whenever Mike is free. Mike is too winded to answer, but Jonathan looks at his watch and makes the appointment. Jonathan's nervous eyes twitch toward Mike, who nods, tries to add something but cannot. The Senator offers his car and chauffeur for their use.

The limousine pulls up to the White House, lets Mike out, and Jonathan climbs into the front seat from the rear seat. The CHAUFFEUR looks at a piece of paper Mike shows him. While driving, the Chauffeur explains to Jonathan the alphabetic arrangement of the streets. As they come to each new street, Jonathan is able to guess the first letter in its name.

The Chauffeur stops at a bar for lunch. The Bartender greets him like a long lost friend, saying that he hasn't seen him for a year. "Diabetes," says the Chauffeur. "Bummer," says the Bartender.

They sit down and order lunch. Jonathan wants a peanut-butter-and-jam sandwich and a glass of milk. The Waitress nods sagely, saying she can handle it. A Friend of the Chauffeur walks over. He is very glad to see the Chauffeur and catch up. He sits down, orders a beer, and asks his buddy what he is drinking. The Chauffeur explains he has diabetes and is not supposed to drink any alcohol, but the Chauffeur's friend says his diabetic brother-in-law is allowed a drink once in a while. As the two argue back and forth, Jonathan slips away with the piece of paper from Mike. He climbs on a bar stool and uses the bar phone to call Linda. In the background, the Friend of the Chauffeur orders two beers from the Waitress. MUSIC PLAYS on the jukebox, drowning out further conversation. Jonathan finds Linda at home and tells her he and the Chauffeur will be over right after lunch.

The Chauffeur opens the front door of the limo for Jonathan. When he gets in, the Chauffeur looks ill. The Friend of the Chauffeur looks out the window at the limo. CAMERA TILTS DOWN to the table and several empty bottles. The limo drives out of frame.

At a signal, signs say all traffic must turn right or left. Inside the limo, the Chauffeur's eyes are swimming. HORNS BLAST him from behind, and the Chauffeur goes full speed ahead into the oncoming one-way traffic. Traffic weaves around the limo, and inside the Chauffeur's eyes close, his head slumps back, and his hands leave the wheel. The limo heads toward a parked car, and Jonathan, climbing over to sit on the Chauffeur's lap, veers the vehicle away. He looks out again and sees an intersection coming up. A SIREN SCREAMS. Jonathan's foot reaches for the brake but can't touch it. The cross traffic gets closer. Finally, Jonathan slides off the lap and the seat, and his foot taps the brake. The car slows down. Then both feet are on the brake, and the car comes to a complete stop right in the middle of a cross street, turned broadside into traffic. Jonathan pulls the hand brake with both hands.

Traffic goes around them. A police car with a flasher parks next to the limo. Cop 1 gets out, walks over, opens the limo door to see Jonathan climbing back up onto the Chauffeur's lap. Cop 1 calls over his partner, Cop 2, who draws a gun and goes over to look at Jonathan smiling up at them. Jonathan reaches for the piece of paper with Linda's address. She and her family live on Lin-ne-an. That's three syllables. And these are only the two-syllable streets. How does he know? asks Cop 1. "Because the names are short," says Jonathan.

Linda's neighborhood. The police car pulls up to Linda's house, where she and Peter are waiting. Cop 1 shakes hands with Jonathan, pins a Police Auxiliary badge on him, and congratulates him. Jonathan gets out and plays with Peter as Cop 1 tells Linda about Jonathan's heroism. She looks at him, and we see her POV—Jonathan and Peter throwing a Frisbee.

National Airport. The limo pulls up. Jonathan and Mike get out and thank the driver. It is the Senator, who says, "That's quite a young man you've got. I know potential when I see it." He drives off as Jonathan looks up at Mike. They walk in.

On the plane, Jonathan is sleeping curled up against Mike and is not sucking his thumb. When their cab pulls up in front of Jonathan's apartment house, it's late in the day and getting dark. Danny is pedaling the toy car on the sidewalk. Jonathan runs to Danny and pulls him over for speeding, showing his badge. Danny wants the badge, offers to trade the car for the badge. Jonathan refuses the car. He wants his badge. It's a *real* badge, he says. Not a toy one. He goes into the building and closes the door.

Observe the differences between the original true experience, the step outline, and the treatment. I remained flexible and listened to the suggestions of my research assistant, Leslie Holland, who liked the story but kept asking questions. One comment she made was that if Jonathan is afraid the men won't like him, his growth can be measured by his ability to hold his own with the senators. So I wrote in the character of the Senator to serve this purpose. After that, I decided to have the driver be the Senator's chauffeur, rather than a cabbie. I saw no advantage in keeping my own character a filmmaker and made Mike a lawyer. Lawyers more routinely meet with senators and White House staff. (If people in the arts cannot transform their experience, then painters would always paint artists and all films would be about filmmakers.)

Once you have examined your treatment and answered the questions on the checklist to your satisfaction, it is time to write the dialogue. By postponing this task until after you have the story, it should be easier to write dialogue that springs out of action. If the character's action is strong and if the situation is strong, dialogue flows more easily. How to write dialogue and some hints about breaking writer's block are covered in the next chapter.

6

Writing
Dialogue

WHAT IS DIALOGUE? How does it differ from real-life conversation? Conversation is the unstructured way people naturally talk. Because people cover their feelings, it often takes days of talking before the hidden agenda—what people really want—begins to emerge. Dialogue, on the other hand, may sound like everyday conversation, but it is really serving to communicate information to the audience so they will have a better understanding and heightened experience of the story and characters.

In this chapter we will be discussing three basic types of dialogue, which have overlapping functions. *Expositional dialogue* explains the status quo and the back story. *Confrontational dialogue* presents a showdown between characters that can reveal their values and background and that helps advance the story. *Logistical dialogue* sets forth a plan that increases tension or laughter in the audience when the plan is foiled. Before we consider each of these in turn, let's take a look at the real meaning behind the words in dialogue, known as the *subtext*.

Subtext

The subtext is the truth behind the words. It is what actors act. Dialogue that says one thing but means another can be compelling, as when the text reads "I hate you" but means "I love you." A graphic example is Rick in *Casablanca* pretending to be interested in Ilse's husband while pining for her, his pain revealed to the audience in close-ups. When you write, you can indicate subtext with one or two words in parentheses. Consider the following scene between a man and woman who have just met. It takes place at night, on a terrace. I am indicating more subtexts than I normally would, just for the sake of illustration.

The couple steal away from the cocktail party.

                    HE
               (continuing)
    I loved that movie.

                    SHE
    Me too. I just love romantic comedies.

She offers him an appetizer.

                    SHE
                (flirting)
    Care for one?

                    HE
           (eating sensuously)
    These appetizers are fine, but I'm getting seriously
    hungry. Are you?

> SHE
> (coy)

I might work up an appetite.

> HE
> (seductively)

If you like sushi, the best place in town is in my neighborhood.

> SHE
> (not ruling out sex)

That might be nice.

> HE
> (pushing)

And the sake is superb.

> SHE
> (toying)

I might have a glass.

> HE
> (pressing)

Or two. They're tiny.

> SHE
> (considering)

We'll see.

Expositional Dialogue

Exposition fills the audience in on the status quo. In the plays of the nineteenth century, the servants would gossip about the master and mistress, thus telling the audience what has happened so far. Modern dialogue writing is more subtle, and characters do not say things to each other solely for the purpose of being overheard. Expositional dialogue also covers the back story—past events that are often suppressed until the drama flushes them out.

To show the impact of the past on the present, many writers use flashbacks. But as I said earlier, the prevailing opinion among filmmakers is that flashbacks slow down the action and suspense. And if a character appears to have no problem in the present, we are not going to empathize with his or her past difficulties for we know all will end well. If the character is to be put in jeopardy, it will have to be in the forward-moving story. Often the past situation that has created a current or impending problem for a character can be revealed through dialogue that sounds like every-day conversation. The audience listens in and gradually learns the back story. They can get this information more quickly through dialogue that is set up as a conflict. During a fight, people naturally review the past when they are verbalizing their versions of remembered actions. Consider the following soap opera–style scene, which begins as a man admits a woman into the living room of his luxurious Park Avenue apartment.

HE

So good to see you. It's been ages.

SHE

I understand you have been seeing a Laura Haines.

HE

Quite so. A very fetching girl.

SHE

You've got to stop seeing her.

HE

But I can't. I love her!

SHE

You *can't* fall in love with her!

HE

Don't tell me you're jealous? After the way you
carried on in Paris! What's to stop me?

SHE

You can't because . . . she's our daughter.

HE

But you never told me anything . . .

SHE

I was too hurt back then in Cannes. I told you I was
off to Africa, but I was really in Brazil with my aunt
while I was pregnant with our baby, now your
girlfriend.

Exposition gets your audience up to speed. When the drama is
ignited and the protagonist meets the opposing forces, you get
into the next kind of dialogue.

Confrontational Dialogue

This is dialogue to be used when there is a clash of values, resulting
in new actions that propel the story forward. The word confrontation seems to imply conflict. What about dialogue where tender
feelings are revealed and there is no conflict? Those scenes frequently come at the end of the film to express the resolution of
conflict. Or they may come during a plateau, setting up the next

confrontation. Rather than create a new type of dialogue called confessional, I will include this kind of dialogue under confrontation. Maybe it will not cover all the cases but I would rather give my readers the impression that open or latent conflict is contained in most confrontational dialogue. The essence of drama is conflict, which does not mean that characters are attacking each other in every line. The conflict could be slow building.

Unlike expositional dialogue early in the film, back story dialogue often comes late in the story. Confrontation often flushes out the back story. For example, when Terry Malloy argues with his brother, Charley, about the past in *On the Waterfront*, they remember the past differently. They say things that have not been said before. The taxi scene dramatically reveals the back story, which explains Terry's lack of loyalty to the crooked union his brother, Charley, represents as an attorney.

Let's tune in at the point when Terry is being bribed with a high-paying do-nothing job in return for his silence before the Waterfront Commission. The brothers discuss the job one evening while riding in a taxi. I am going to abridge the scene slightly.

                    CHARLEY
There's a slot for a boss loader on the new pier we're opening up.

                    TERRY
                  (interested)
Boss loader!

                    CHARLEY
Ten cents a hundred pounds for everything that moves in and out. And you don't have to lift a

finger. It'll be three, four hundred a week just for openers.

TERRY

For all that dough I ain't got to do nothing?

CHARLEY

Absolutely nothing. You do nothing and you say nothing. You understand, don't you, kid.

TERRY

(struggling with an unfamiliar problem of
conscience and loyalties)

Yeah—yeah—I guess I do—but there's a lot more to this thing than I originally thought.

CHARLEY

You don't mean you're thinking of testifying against—

(turns a thumb in toward himself)

TERRY

I don't know—I don't know! I tell you I ain't made up my mind yet. That's what I wanted to talk to you about.

CHARLEY

(patiently, as to a stubborn child)

Listen, Terry, these piers we handle through the local—you know what they're worth to us?

TERRY

I know. I know.

CHARLEY

Well, then you know Cousin Johnny isn't going to
jeopardize a setup like that for one rubber-lipped—

TERRY

(simultaneous)

Don't say that!

CHARLEY

(continuing)

ex-tanker who's walking on his heels—?

TERRY

Don't say that!

CHARLEY

What the hell!!!

TERRY

I could have been better!

CHARLEY

Listen, that's not the point.

TERRY

I could have been better!

CHARLEY

That skunk I got to manage you brought you along
too fast.

TERRY

It wasn't him!

(years of abuse crying out in him)

It was you, Charley. You and Johnny. Like the night

the two of youse come in the dressing room and says, 'Kid, this ain't your night—we're going for the price on Wilson.' *It ain't my night.* I'd of taken Wilson apart that night. I was ready—remember the early rounds throwing them combinations. So what happens—this bum Wilson he gets the title shot—outdoors in the ball park!—and what do I get—a couple of bucks and a one-way ticket to Palookaville.

    (more and more aroused as he relives it)

It was you, Charley. You was my brother. You should have looked out for me. Instead of making me take them dives for the short-end money.

CHARLEY

I always had a bet down for you. You saw some money.

TERRY

You don't understand! I could've been a contender. I could've had class and been somebody. Real class. Instead of a bum, let's face it, which is what I am. It was you, Charley.

Charley takes a long, fond look at Terry. Then he glances quickly out the window.

The back story that is included in this confrontational dialogue reveals Terry's motivation for betraying the union and testifying before the congressional committee. Terry's suppressed value—his reputation—has always yielded to his brother's value of loyalty to the corrupt union. Buried feelings on each side have been aired, and a change is beginning to occur, as it should in every scene. The only way that Terry can regain his reputation is through his testimony before the Waterfront Commission.

Let's look at another scene—this time from the previously mentioned short *The Last Days of Hope and Time*, directed by Andrew Wagner. It is another confrontation scene that flushes out the back story. But it is a also a present-day conflict of values—the values of Albert Lee against those of his wife, Dee. Albert Lee, once a high school basketball star, is "the greatest player never to have played in the NBA." His arrogance always drove away the teams that had intended to recruit him. The subsequent lockout has left him still trying to recover his dream every day on the basketball court in the park. His wife wants him to get a job, support his family, and be a role model to his son.

The showdown takes place after Albert Lee fails to go on a job interview that Dee has set up for him. He was in fact leaving the playground to keep this appointment when Butch, a rival who actually played pro ball and became a ten-time NBA All-star, asked him to stay and play. They end up playing until early evening. As they disperse, Dee confronts Albert in the playground with a contemptuous look. We pick up the scene as they enter their home.

INT. ALBERT'S HOUSE—NIGHT
They both enter.

> DEE
>
> How do you think that makes me look? Practically on my knees. '*Please* give him a job. He wants it. He's reliable.' Ain't that why your son stayed out of school today? Following your example, playing in the park the rest of his life.

Albert goes upstairs to wash up in the bathroom.

ALBERT

Whit Jefferson—one of the all time greats—only two years out of the league. I demolished him. Sent him crawling.

Albert seems to have the last word until Dee suddenly starts.

DEE

I sure hope Butch wasn't too shook up to drive his 450 SL convertible. I hope he made it safely back to his three-story house on Malibu Beach.

ALBERT

You know what your problem is? . . . You are too materialistic. You need to develop your spiritual side. It ain't the size of your house that matters. It's the size of your heart. You talk about me being an example to my son. I'll teach him how to care. I'll teach him how to be a friend to a friend.

DEE

Teach him how to read?

ALBERT

Teach him not to be no educated fool. Plenty of folks can read. But not the crook in the three-piece suit that's cheating them out of their future.

DEE

You are so street smart! *You're* no educated fool. Nobody's gonna tell you how to do your thing. You don't need the NBA. You don't need somebody—

just the feeling. But when they say 'Fine, go back to the playground,' suddenly you're this misunderstood boy that they—they—*they* blackballed. Which is it, Albert? Who are you really? Cowboy or boy?

At this Albert sits next to his son, takes the book he is reading about the myth of Sisyphus, who was punished in hell by pushing a rock up a hill and watching it eternally roll down the hill once it is on top. He reads aloud like a third grader.

As the story continues, Dee leaves Albert and takes their daughter with her. Albert Lee begins a job assisting his high school basketball coach. When this happens, Dee comes back.

Both characters advance their values until the end, when the back story comes up. Dee knows—but the rest of the family does not—that Albert Lee had his chance in pro ball on several teams, but his arrogance got in the way. The truth is only hinted at, but we can assume it took the form of the same egocentricity that we saw on the basketball court when two players on the sidelines say that he never passes the ball.

Logistical Dialogue

The third type of dialogue, logistical, sounds as if the writer is imitating normal planning conversation. Here is an example.

HE

Why don't we have lunch? I'd like to know you better.

SHE

That's totally possible. When's good for you?

HE

Saturday's okay. Oh, wait a minute. I think I have something then.

SHE

Why don't we make it Sunday?

HE

I can't do lunch but I can do breakfast.

SHE

Great.

HE

Officers Club. 8:30. See you then.

Not exactly dramatic, is it? Under normal circumstances, I would suggest cutting all dialogue after the line "I'd like to get to know you better" and moving directly to a scene in which the two are breakfasting at the officers club. But if we make some tiny— but significant—changes to the original scene, it can be very tense. In the background as they talk is a calendar that indicates the conversation takes place on Friday, December 5, 1941. The camera tilts down to napkins that read Pearl Harbor Officers Club. Now the same turgid dialogue has an ironic and dramatic meaning. The audience is going to be rooting for them not to pick Sunday and worried that they will both be killed. Context is everything.

Another kind of logistical dialogue that can work is that which misleads the audience about how a scene will go. The difference between plan and actuality generates either tension or laughter. Such scenes are frequent in caper films. First comes the setup, then the execution, where everything starts to go wrong. The difference between the two puts the participants in jeopardy, creating suspense and entertainment.

One more note about dialogue: When you start the first draft of your script, you might want to do it in stages. First let the words spill onto the page or computer screen as fast as possible. You can, if you like, use the characters' initials rather than their names and begin each line flush left instead of centered on the page. But I strongly recommend that you impose the screenplay format on your work before showing it to a teacher, a fellow student, or even a friend—and especially before anyone in the film or TV business sees it. If the form is wrong, your script will look amateurish and the reader will have less respect for the work.

The origin of the rigid professional format is economic. Production personnel need to study the script and know quickly how much it is going to cost. Interior scenes cost more than exterior scenes. In the old studio system, capitalizing FX (sound effects) or MUSIC alerted the various departments to their tasks.

Now let's take a closer look at screenplay format.

7

Screenplay Format

THE FORMAT DEMONSTRATED HERE is known as the *master scene form*, a master scene being one that shows all the action. It is used for a *reading script*. In this type of script, the various types of camera shots are not specified unless they have significance for the drama. Later, the director of the film creates what is called a *shooting script*, which includes all the camera shots and production notes, and has a number assigned to each scene. But do not burden your reading script with such details.

Some Basic Rules

Here are some rules to get you started. Before each scene, indicate whether it will take place indoors or outdoors by writing in caps either INT., for interiors, or EXT., for exteriors. Then name the location and time of day in a few words. Do not make your location labels colorful. Rather than say A SPARKLING BROOK IN A VERDANT MEADOW, use BROOK IN A MEADOW and save the adjectives for the scene description on the next line. Time of day can be general (DAY or NIGHT) or more specific (LATER or SUNSET).

An example that includes all three elements would be INT. BERTHA'S HOUSE—DAY. Once you are inside the house and you change the location to the kitchen, you simply have to say INT. KITCHEN. We assume the story is in the same location at the same time of day unless otherwise indicated.

As noted, you do not have to put scene numbers in now. Those can wait until you are ready for the film to be produced. Then they will be vital because the crew, when planning or shooting, will be referring to scenes by number.

Anything to do with titles, such as TITLES BEGIN or TITLES END, is in caps. The same goes for MUSIC BEGINS, MUSIC UP, or MUSIC OUT. Put each character's name in caps the first time you use it in scene descriptions, and use initial caps thereafter. With nonspeaking roles in which the characters are not named, use initial caps and labels such as Janitor, Porter, Waiter. I do not advocate writing CUT TO after every scene. Although this is still advocated in some textbooks, it is not standard practice in Hollywood and is not necessary.

In the opening of your screenplay, introduce your main characters with a short, deftly worded description:

A couple spread a blanket under the shade of a tree and put down their picnic basket. MILLICENT, 30, a serious lawyer, pours some wine as VIRGIL, 32, a devil-may-care airline pilot, takes the picnic lunch from the basket. MUSIC UP. SUPER TITLES.

The description of the action, camera moves, and so forth, should be written in a literate but compact style meant to capture the reader's interest. You can introduce important characters with a phrase or two, as above. The age of the character is often left vague because the age range indicated is the first step in casting. Many actors are very sensitive about age. "Late forties" will get the attention of an actress sooner than "early fifties," and yet the look on-screen may be the same.

Camera Instructions

Capitalize camera instructions such as PAN (move laterally); TILT (move vertically); BOOM UP or BOOM DOWN (camera rises or lowers by hydraulic movement); DOLLY IN or DOLLY BACK (camera moves closer or farther away); and ZOOM IN or ZOOM BACK. Do not write a lot of camera directions because they impede reading. In addition, if someone else directs your script, the director will find them unnecessary, maybe patronizing, like a landlord who leaves too many notes for a tenant. The director has to discover the script on his or her own. Save camera directions for dramatic moments or for situations where it would be too difficult to understand the story without them.

If it is essential for the reader of your script to picture the nuances of close-ups and eye contact, you can indicate close-ups with caps:

ON MARIA [This indicates that in the final editing sequence, the screen shows Maria]
Noticing JEFF, a new employee.

JEFF
Removing shirt, revealing muscular chest, putting on apron.

FULL SHOT
Maria carries a tray of dishes toward him.

JEFF
Ogling her. Attracted.

MARIA
Blushing.

From time to time, you will find it necessary to indicate that your character is undergoing a *dawning realization*. At each stage of awareness, you might want to use a close-up of the character, then cut to what he or she has just become aware of:

INT. ABANDONED BUILDING—NIGHT

Patrick enters, hears Annette screaming.

PATRICK
I'm here. You're safe.

We can HEAR her FOOTSTEPS coming down the staircase.

CLOSE ON PATRICK

WHAT HE SEES

As soon as she rounds the corner, the staircase becomes shaky, starts to crumble. She steps back. Rapist grabs her.

Once you finish describing eye contact, dawning realizations, or other kinds of close-ups, you can return to the master scene style by writing FULL SHOT, WHOLE SCENE, or BACK TO SCENE.

Lab Effects, Sound Effects, and Music

Lab effects, such as DISSOLVE TO, FADE IN, FADE OUT, and SLOMO (slow motion), are included, when appropriate, in the scene description. Dissolves and fades are indicated on the right side of the page. Also put in capital letters significant sounds such as footsteps, thunder, and dramatic sounds, using the abbreviation for sound effects, FX (e.g., FX: SAFE OPENING). When it comes to music descriptions, don't bog the script down by constantly pulling in your favorite music. Nor is it necessary to include expensive special effects. In your first draft you should be selling your reader on the story.

Dialogue and Page Format

When writing dialogue, center the name of the character and below the name put in a word or two of subtext instructions, which can be centered or positioned just to the left beneath the character's name. Indent the margins on either side of the centered dialogue about twenty spaces. At crucial points of the dialogue, you can insert parenthetical descriptions, as in the following:

> MELISSA
> I was a happy child. I used to love to race my horse
> in the fields . . .
> (choking up)
> . . . until one day I ran across my father and a neighbor kissing.

But if the interpolation is lengthy, it should be presented flush left and without the parentheses:

> MELISSA
> I was a happy child. I used to love to race my horse
> in the fields . . .

Unable to continue, she gets up, finds a tissue and comes back, composes herself.

> MELISSA (CONTD)
> . . . until one day I ran across my father and a neighbor kissing.

Try to use a few deft strokes of minimal language, compressing the essence of the action. Here are some pages from a screenplay of mine to illustrate the format further.

EXT. FEDERAL PRISON—DAY

A cab pulls up. JACK WILKINS, 45, emerges with his briefcase and enters the security office as handcuffed Prisoners are being led into a van. TITLES BEGIN.

INT. SECURITY STATION—DAY

TITLES CONTINUE OVER A MONTAGE OF SECURITY PROCEDURES.

INT. PRISON LAVATORY—DAY

A Lookout is posted at the door. Inside, a three-card monte game is in progress with one Dealer, two Players, and PATRICK LAWRENCE, 40, who peeks around the stall corner while brushing a toilet. He is patrician, calculating, reserved. The Dealer finishes shuffling the cards.

> PATRICK
> (tossing quarter)
Middle card.

                         FIRST PLAYER
                        (handing quarter)
    This side.

The Dealer overturns the cards. The ace of spades is on the
side where the First Player bet. The Lookout snaps his
fingers. The Dealer collects his cards, pays the winner, and
leaves. The First Player opens his fly and addresses the
urinal. Patrick mops his way toward him. MUSIC UP.

A few final words about page format. Center the page number
at the bottom of the page. If your character is talking and you
reach the end of the page (represented by dotted lines), use the
following format:

                          GUARD
        Your lawyer's here. Your hearing's about to

    .... (page break) ....

                      GUARD (CONTD)
        begin any minute.

    If the page break comes in the middle of a scene description, do
the following:

INT. CORRIDOR

The two men walk toward the end of a locked corridor. The

    .... (page break) ....

CONTD

Guard unlocks the door and ushers Patrick to the other side
of the door.

For some variations on the master scene format, I recommend
Professional Writer's Teleplay/Screenplay Format by Jerome Coopersmith, a professor of screenwriting at Hunter College and an
experienced writer for TV. His manual also will tell you how to
copyright your full-length script and register it with the Writers
Guild of America. The booklet is available only from the Writers
Guild East, 555 West 57th Street, New York, NY 10019;
212-767-7800.

Now that we have looked at the mechanics of a script, which
not only tells the film's story but also serves as a production guide,
it is time to deal with the first draft.

8

████████████████

Writing
the First
Draft

IF ACTION IS DRIVING the dialogue—that is, if the characters have sharply defined goals—it's a lot easier to write dialogue. Nevertheless, some people have problems writing dialogue at first, so the following hints may be helpful.

Develop the Voice

Read your character profiles, particularly the voice, before you write the scene, so you can review how the people talk. For example, if one character is a race car driver, he might accuse his girlfriend of sideswiping him all the time. When exasperated with her, he might say that he has finally hit the wall: "The car's on fire. I'm climbing out." Develop the imagery by listing words and phrases that each of your characters might use.

Objects Symbolize Values

Decide the issues that stand between the characters. What values is each fighting for? Make lists of how these values are expressed—in words and in objects that symbolize these values. For instance, a man whose wife is overspending might hold up the latest dress she bought. What he does next will depend on his character. One man might take the dress back to the store; another would rip it up; still another would ask his wife to model it because he loves her regardless of how much she spends. The dress is not just a purchase. It represents her lifestyle, self-image, dream, which may or may not be incompatible with his.

Let's go back to the racer and his girl arguing. Suppose she wants him to give up racing, and he wants to continue. She gets hold of the keys to his racing car and threatens to throw them into the incinerator. Then she actually does. In retrieving them, he burns his hand, which prevents him from racing for a while. Suppose someone else drives his car and is killed in an explosion meant for him. Suddenly, this is not a verbal clash of values. It is . . . cinema. Verbal clashes are for plays, which are often clarifications of the past when pigeons come home to roost. In films, the action is always going forward in the present tense.

Shape the Scene

Decide where your characters stand at the beginning of the scene and how they have changed by the scene's end. There should be such a shift in at least one of the characters. At the end of the taxi scene in *On the Waterfront* (see chapter 6), Charley just stares out the taxi window. What is he feeling? Guilt? Resignation? We don't know right away. But a couple of scenes later he is found murdered. Perhaps he knows that Terry has to betray the union to restore his dignity and self-esteem. Perhaps he feels guilty for making Terry throw the fight. Perhaps he knows he'll be killed if he cannot prevent his brother from testifying. At the end of the scene, both characters are different.

Use Terms as Shorthand

Find language that represents the way each character sees the problem. A term often becomes a ball that one character tosses at another, who tosses it back. The girlfriend of the race car driver says:

> SHE
>
> We have to work on *us*—the way you treat me.

> HE
>
> I've learned there comes a time when you can't tinker any more with an engine. It either works or it doesn't.

> SHE
>
> You're not going to even open the hood—poke around, tinker a *little* bit before you junk it?

Tinker, in this case, takes on the meaning that lies at the heart of the scene. The characters must work on the relationship or forget it. He wants to discard the alliance, like a machine that does not work.

In *Casablanca*, Rick does not say to Ilse, "We can always remember back to the time when we were lovers in France without anything spoiling it, when it was just us and the world did not intrude." He says, "We'll always have Paris."

Pay Off Dialogue with Action

When you get to the end of the scene, don't conclude it with one person verbally conceding to the other. End the scene with the two characters separating, and then write the conclusion with action. Let's say that after the argument between the race car driver and his girlfriend, the man stalks out of the motel where they're spending the night, gets into his car, and drives off, leaving her in tears. He is driving along when he looks into the rearview mirror and sees a flash cut of her face. We see a long shot where he pulls to the side of the road and pauses, then makes a U-turn and drives back to the motel. We don't have to see him park and knock on the door. We can cut to the clinch.

Use Foreshadowing

Foreshadowing is planting seeds in the beginning of the action that at first do not seem to be significant. But later they erupt into dramatic events. In my own script about Jonathan, his driving of a toy car becomes the forerunner of the scene where he grabs the wheel of the real car. When events in the film come together, it is very satisfying to an audience.

Convert Dialogue to Action

When you have finished a draft, the next step is very important. Examine your dialogue for actions buried within speeches. If you are like my typical student, you will write scenes where people sit around and argue with one another, referring to events offscreen. This is what happens in a dormitory and on TV sitcoms, but it cannot happen in a short. A conversation might serve as the first draft of a scene, but do not stop there. Consider the following scene:

INT. DORMITORY ROOM—DAY

TREVOR is studying at his desk when DON rushes in, locks the door, and collapses into an armchair.

> DON
>
> Boy, that was close.

> TREVOR
>
> What happened?

Don gets a beer from the refrigerator, opens it.

> DON
>
> I'm trying to be, like, Mr. Nice Guy. I see this kind of pathetic street person, you know, and I say to myself, what the hell, give him a quarter. The guy's not doing too well, see, most people are passing him by, you know, like they're looking the other way, cause he's kind of ugly. So I fish out a quarter and I give it to him and—guess what? He won't take it! He hands it back to me, and he says he's an addict and he didn't want to go hit some old lady over the head. He wants to turn himself over to a rehab center, but the center's in the country and he needs transportation money, see.

> TREVOR
>
> Didn't you tell him about the center a block from here at St. Joe's?

> DON
>
> I told him, but he says it's no good and he'll only go back to drugs. . . . I give him four quarters, and he hands them back to me. He looks at me and damned if he doesn't start crying. Not just one tear running down his cheek. But he's practically boo-hooing at me, and he says I'm forcing him to hit some old lady over the head. I start to leave, and he gets up and starts arguing with me, calling me names.
>
> TREVOR
>
> Like what?

People write scenes like this because they are influenced by TV sitcoms, which are one-set shows often performed before a live audience. The same characters play scenes on the same set week after week. As mentioned earlier, this is done for reasons of economy. I am in no way putting down the sitcom. It is often written and produced at a very sophisticated level, and many fine cinema artists, such as Garry Marshall, Penny Marshall, Rob Reiner, and Ron Howard, have emerged from this background. All I am saying is that a sitcom is not cinematic.

Let's now try to put the offstage event into a cinematic scene.

EXT. SUBWAY ENTRANCE—LATE DAY

DON, 20, emerges, carrying his book bag, wearing his school jacket.

DON'S POV

HOMELESS MAN

Sitting on sidewalk, leaning against a bldg. He MOANS and talks to himself. Pedestrians pass him. One notices him but is put off by the MOANING. He keeps on walking.

DON

Noticing him, reaching for a coin.

CLOSER ON HOMELESS MAN

Noticing Don's stare, returning it.

BACK TO SCENE

Don drops a quarter into the Homeless Man's paper cup.

> HOMELESS MAN
> Hey, can I talk to you?

> DON
> Sure.

He hands Don back his quarter.

> DON
> How come?

> HOMELESS MAN
> Because this ain't enough to keep me from doing what I got to do.

> DON
> What's that?

> HOMELESS MAN
> I'm an addict. You know what that's like?

Don reaches into his pocket and hands him four quarters.

CLOSE ON HOMELESS MAN

Shakes his head. Tears form. He looks up as if Don wronged him. He hands the quarters back.

> HOMELESS MAN
> You don't get it, do you? I need to go to a rehab center outside the city. I need transportation. I need twenty bucks.

WHOLE SCENE

Don moves away. Pedestrians walk toward them.

CLOSER ON PEDESTRIANS

A Middle-aged Woman, carrying her purse on her shoulder.

> HOMELESS MAN
> This is on *your* conscience, man. Not mine.

He takes the Middle-aged Woman's bag and runs. Don starts to chase him, but the man goes down the stairs leading to the subway.

INT. SUBWAY

Don chases him down the stairs as a train arrives. The Homeless Man hops the turnstile, but Don goes to buy a token. By the time he goes through the turnstile, the Homeless Man is on the subway and the doors have closed.

The short is off and running now. I don't know how it progresses, but I have the feeling Don has not seen the last of the Homeless Man.

Dealing with Writer's Block

What do you do if you're stuck? You sit staring at a blank piece of paper or a blank computer screen. You go to the refrigerator. You pick up the crossword puzzle, but when you've finished it, the page or screen is still blank and you feel even more guilty. You start calling yourself names—untalented, blocked, dilettantish. You may suffer from a paralyzing kind of perfectionism where you expect the writing to be perfect from the very start. But the fact is that writing can be clumsy, disorganized, and unimaginative at first. The rule to follow is: "Don't get it right. Get it written." Then structure it.

Maybe you're having problems with concentration. What can you do? Sit down to write at the same time every day. For me it has to be early in the morning, but for you it might be ten in the evening. Turn off the phone, and don't get up for at least an hour. If you write nothing, simply stop and come back at the same time tomorrow. Write down fragments. They will turn into sentences, then scenes, and suddenly words will start to flow. Maybe not right away but eventually the story will pour out—particularly if it comes from your own experiences.

You might want to free up your mind with meditation. To acquire this skill, you can read *The Relaxation Response* by Herbert Benson, a Harvard Medical School cardiologist, or learn other types of meditation such as Syda Yoga and Transcendental Meditation, by taking courses.

Make a Commitment to the Script

The more committed you are to your script, the better you will write. The following poem by Goethe is worth thinking about, maybe even framing for your wall:

Until one is committed, there is hesitancy,
the chance to draw back,
always ineffectiveness.
Concerning all acts of initiative
there is one elementary truth,
the ignorance of which kills
countless ideas and endless plans:
That the moment one definitely commits
oneself, then providence moves too.
All sorts of things occur to help one.
A whole stream of events issues from the
decision, raising in one's favor all manner of
unforeseen incidents and meetings and
material assistance which no man
could have dreamed would come his way.
Whatever you can do or
dream you can, begin it!
Boldness has genius, power and magic in it.

9

Testing
the
Script

I REMEMBER READING AN INTERVIEW with Neil Simon in which he said that when he shows a script to a producer, he is equally prepared for one of two reactions—that it is the greatest play in the English language, or it is the worst piece of garbage the producer has ever read. Of course, Neil Simon is a model rewriter. Gene Saks recalled that if he was directing a Neil Simon play and a scene was not working during rehearsals, Saks would reassure Simon that he could get it to work. But Simon would leave the theater and produce a new scene before Saks could rework it. Simon has no ego about his work before it is presented to an audience. And you shouldn't either. Keep an open mind as you show your final first draft to others.

The Reading

Even if you are not writing in a classroom setting and do not have a ready-made audience, there is a method of getting feedback before you plunge into production. Invite friends in to hear your script read and to engage in a group discussion of its strengths and weaknesses. Afterwards, serve refreshments.

If possible, have someone besides yourself read the scene descriptions. Edit them down so the audience can get the story flow. If you have a cast in mind for the film, ask them to read the various parts. If not, bring in some friends who read well; since they will be reading for sense, they will not be expected to turn in a polished performance. You can even have a rehearsal sometime beforehand or right before the reading. Just make sure you have proofed your script at least twice before you show it to anyone. Typos and misspellings are distracting to a reader. Instead of thinking about your script, he or she will be focusing on your sloppiness.

Ask someone to be in charge of the discussion. This individual should encourage people to be critical. If I am coordinating a reading of someone else's script, in or out of class, to get the ball rolling I usually invite people to speak up by raising questions about how they liked the script and each of the characters. Once top-of-the-head opinions are voiced, I try to focus the audience on what the work is all about—the controlling idea, mentioned earlier—to see if they experience what the author intended.

I also ask the audience whether they believe the essence of the script, and I try to get them to point out to the author what they have a hard time believing. I ask whether the premise is strong and unusual. I ask whether the protagonist is sympathetic and what can be done to increase sympathy. Similarly with the antagonist: Is he or she unsympathetic?

If your own script is being discussed, listen carefully and do not inhibit the feedback process by looking injured. Try to look positive even when people are saying hurtful things, dismissing work that you toiled over. You won't remember much of what is said, so it's a good idea to tape-record the feedback. Then the next day you can begin to sort out people's reactions.

After a reading of a screenplay about my adolescence, I asked twenty people to participate in a discussion of the script. I did not take part in the discussion, but I tape-recorded it. Then I asked people to fill out the accompanying form while food was being served.

Homefront Feedback

Please jot down some notes on the following questions:

Did you care about David?

What would make you care more?

Did you care about Sarah?

What would make you care more?

Do you have any comments about any other characters?

Brenda

Danforth

Trudy

O'Brian

Joan

Morris

Mrs. Nelson

Esther

Perry

Can you think of any stars for these roles?

Was anything unclear?

What did you find unbelievable?

What did you find funny?

Unfunny?

Did anything offend you?

Where did your interest flag?

Which turns in the story seemed predictable?

Did the script ever seem trite?

What would make the script better?

The comments from those who filled out the form helped me enormously as I worked on the next draft.

A final word about evaluating the tape-recorded discussion of your script. You will find that reactions can eventually be placed in one of two categories:

Minority reports: Eccentric opinions that no one else agrees with. Ignore these unless something in the minority report strikes a chord with you.

Consensus opinions: If close to a majority of people seem to be criticizing the same things in different words, then this criticism should be heeded. Try to summarize *their* opinion in *your* words. Try to hone in on what is missing or what is excessive. Most writers overstate their point because they are afraid audiences will not get their message. So repetition is natural even in a final first draft. You have to let the garden grow before you prune.

Completing the Script for
Jonathan's Turn

What follows is my script for *Jonathan's Turn*, which you have seen progress from anecdote to step outline to treatment. My assistant, Leslie Holland, and my cinematographer, Ross Lowell, gave me excellent feedback that resulted in changes at every stage. You will note that I eliminated the Thanksgiving Day parade—I did not want to wait until November to make the film. In chapter 15, "Producing *Jonathan's Turn*," you will see how the script was changed further because the airlines were uncooperative.

I begin with a title page, which every final script should have.

JONATHAN'S TURN

by

Ed Levy

WGA* Registered

* Writers Guild of America

INT. JONATHAN'S APT.—UPPER WEST SIDE NEW YORK CITY—DAY

CLOSE ON JONATHAN

A serious, handsome boy of 6, he is seen through holes in the tower of blocks he is building. His concentration is total as he cautiously adds another block to the top.

ANOTHER ANGLE

Jonathan continues building as CAMERA PANS to Jonathan's problem, his brother, DANNY, 5, devilish and rebellious, playing with a less interesting toy. Danny looks over enviously at Jonathan, then crawls over to him, takes a couple of blocks, and starts to "improve" Jonathan's tower.

> JONATHAN
> Don't! You'll ruin it!

This does not stop Danny, who puts the blocks on top. All the blocks fall down. Danny nearly dies laughing.

> JONATHAN
> You see! Play with your own toys. Pleeease.

Danny begins to WAIL. Finally, some words emerge.

> DANNY
> Moooom-ma MAAAA-MAA!

Danny immediately goes into a deep WAIL, which draws his MOTHER from the kitchen. She carries a paintbrush

and wears a smock. We see mostly her legs since this entire
film is SHOT FROM JONATHAN'S POV.

>   MOTHER
>   What's wrong *now*, Danny?

>   DANNY
>   He won't let me help.

>   MOTHER
>   Let him help you, Jonathan.

>   JONATHAN
>   He just crashed the whole tower.

>   DANNY
>   (crying)
>   I want to build a house for you.

>   MOTHER
>   Give him a turn, Jonathan.

Danny beams. Jonathan makes a face and charges into the
kitchen.

INT. KITCHEN

Jonathan sits at the kitchen table and angrily covers his head
with his hands. The Mother goes back to her easel.

EXT. JONATHAN'S BLDG.*

---

* Abbreviate as much as possible words like: BLDG. (building), BGD
(background), FGD (foreground), POV (point of view), VO (voice-over),
CU (close-up).

MIKE, 35, father of the boys, enters the bldg.

INT. LOBBY

Mike approaches Doorman, who looks up the intercom number for the boys' apartment.

INT. KITCHEN

CU intercom phone ringing. PULL BACK as Jonathan runs to phone but cannot reach it. Danny enters, pushes a chair under the phone, climbs it, and answers. Jonathan has been aced again.

> DANNY
> Hello . . . hi, Daddy . . . OK.
> (to Jonathan)
> Daddy's here.

JONATHAN

Angry. Aced again.

INT. APT. REAR DOOR

Mother opens the door for them, kisses them good-bye. Jonathan turns his cheek.

> MOTHER
> Tell your father that next weekend I want to take you to my mother's. And don't be so grumpy, Jonathan.

Door closes.

INT. ELEVATOR

The boys are riding. Suddenly, Danny blurts out.

> DANNY
>
> Grumpy! Bumpy!

Danny sticks out his tongue.

> JONATHAN
>
> Baby! Clumsy baby!

Danny sticks out his tongue even farther.

> DANNY
>
> Grumpy! Dumpy! Bumpy!

INT. JONATHAN'S BLDG. LOBBY

The elevator door opens. Mike is waiting. Jonathan jumps into his arms. He carries him toward a chandelier.

CHANDELIER

Mike walks into frame with Jonathan on his shoulders. Jonathan TINKLES the chandelier. They start to turn away when Danny WAILS. Mike puts down Jonathan, picks up Danny, who swings the chandelier back and forth until pieces of it can be HEARD falling. Mike moves away.

DOORMAN

Scandalized by Danny, he takes a whisk broom and pan, moves toward them, glowering.

CHANDELIER AREA

Mike is picking up large pieces of glass. When the Doorman

comes, scowling, Mike deposits his shards in the dustpan and they leave.

EXT.—TOY STORE

Mike exits the store with a gift-wrapped package, which he hands to Danny to carry. Danny wants to be carried on Mike's shoulders. Jonathan lingers at a pedal car in the window.

THE CAR

It gleams back at him.

JONATHAN

His thumb goes into his mouth. Mike's hand reaches down to him and coaxes him away. When they exit, the CAMERA REFRAMES for the car.

INT. APT. ENTRANCE—DAY

At Jonathan's eye level, we see a door pulled open by a Hostess who takes the present and puts party hats on the boys. She hands Danny a whistle that blows out a rolled-up tongue of paper and makes a noise when it retracts. Immediately, he runs inside and charges toward a couple of four-year-olds with the same whistles. They begin fighting.

JONATHAN

Feeling lost. Mike's hand leads him away to LINDA, 35, and her son, PETER, 6.

> MIKE'S VOICE
> Come on. I want you to meet your cousins. Hi, Linda. How are you?

They are kissing out of frame, covering and then revealing Jonathan, who is seen between them. He is looking up, taking everything in.

> MIKE'S VOICE
> This is cousin Linda . . .

> LINDA'S VOICE
> . . . and this is your cousin Peter—from Washington.

Her hand guides Peter, who is pleased to find a cousin. Jonathan pulls Mike's sleeve. Mike bends down, and Jonathan whispers:

> JONATHAN
> What's a cousin?

> MIKE
> It's like a brother. But you don't live with him.

Jonathan is intrigued. He goes over to Peter with a big smile.

> PETER
> Want to see my watch?

They huddle together. Peter shows how it works. A Mime in costume brushes by them. APPLAUSE when he enters the adjoining living room. Peter puts the watch on Jonathan's wrist. A wall of adults forms at the back of the room. Jonathan tries to see through the legs as LAUGHTER erupts from the other room. Jonathan reaches out his arms, asking his father to lift him so he can see.

WHAT JONATHAN SEES

A MIME entertains the crowd, doing an impression of walking the dog.

MIKE AND JONATHAN

Mike lifts Jonathan above the crowd to see the Mime.

THE MIME

Imitates dog sniffing a hydrant. Suddenly, the WAIL of Danny can be heard. The Mime holds his ear to the horrible NOISE. He pretends to drop the leash to put his hands over his ears. He picks it up again. The WAIL starts up again. He hands the leash and the dog to a child and goes over to Danny, as the screams continue. The mime wails with open mouth and knotted-up face in sync with Danny. He goes through the crowd and takes Danny over to the top of a piano and places him there. He widens his own mouth into a smile and then does the same with Danny.

JONATHAN

Laughing. Glad to see Danny put in his place.

INT. HALLWAY OUTSIDE APT.

Linda walks the threesome to the elevator. CAMERA IS STILL AT THE BOYS' LEVEL.

LINDA

When are you coming to Washington?

MIKE

It's hard to predict.

> LINDA

Bring Jonathan when you come.

Jonathan smiles. Jonathan hands back Peter's watch.

> MIKE

I guess I could do that.

> LINDA

I'll meet your plane, and Jonathan can spend the day with Peter.

Peter jumps up and down. Peter imitates the Mime being a dog at a hydrant. Jonathan giggles. They both imitate the Mime. Elevator arrives.

> MIKE

Wonderful to see you.

Quick kisses all around. The threesome gets on elevator. Elevator door closes.

EXT. TOY STORE—DAY

Mike is carrying out a wrapped package. The boys are jumping up and down with excitement.

EXT. RIVERSIDE PARK OR STRAWBERRY FIELDS

Mike is assembling a toy car with his Swiss Army knife. He runs the car back and forth to make sure everything is okay. The two boys vie to be the first in.

> DANNY

Me first! Me first!

MIKE

I want you boys to share this.
(Danny gets in and pedals off)
Danny come back here! . . . Danny!

Mike notices a Street Vendor selling watches at a nearby table. He goes over to the table.

MIKE

How much are these watches?

STREET VENDOR

Ten bucks.

Mike takes two, gives him a twenty. In the distance, Danny looks back, and Mike waves the watch. Mike gives Jonathan his watch to put on. Danny speeds back.

MIKE

(handing Danny his watch)
I don't want you to fight over this car. Each boy gets ten minutes on it, and then you have to switch. The big hand goes two numbers. If you start at the two, you stop at the . . . what?

DANNY

Three.

JONATHAN

Four!

MIKE

Let's let Jonathan go first, and you be the time-keeper. Have you ever been a timekeeper before?

> DANNY

I'll be the timekeeper and the driver too.

Jonathan gets into the car, drives off.

> MIKE
> (to Danny)

Now show me where the big hand will be when you get a turn with the car.

> DANNY

It will be right here.

> MIKE

Almost right.

OVERALL SHOT

Danny and Mike confer on the watch. Jonathan drives away and back.

INT. JONATHAN'S KITCHEN

MOTHER

We HEAR boys arguing about whose turn it is. She puts down her paintbrush and puts in earplugs.

INT. LIVING ROOM

FULL SHOT

Danny riding the car. PULL BACK to see Jonathan looking at his watch.

> JONATHAN

It is *so* my turn.

DANNY

It's not ten minutes yet.

JONATHAN

It's twelve. Let me see your watch.

INT. LIVING ROOM

DANNY (VO)

Something happened to it.

CU DANNY'S WATCH

The crystal is shattered. The watch is unreadable.

JONATHAN

You broke it. That's what happened.

DANNY

I didn't. It just happened.

Jonathan gets into the car and drives away. Danny WAILS.

MOTHER

Enters with an icepack on her head.

MOTHER

Jonathan, let him have the car. I can't take the noise.

JONATHAN

Dad says we should take turns.

MOTHER

But he doesn't have my headache.

Jonathan gets out of the car, marches to the kitchen.

INT. KITCHEN

Jonathan reaches up to the phone and touch-dials a number.

INT. MIKE'S OFFICE

Mike's intercom BUZZES. He picks it up.

> SECRETARY (VO)
> Your son Jonathan, Mr. Altman.

> MIKE
> (picking up)
> Jonathan?

INT. JONATHAN'S KITCHEN

> JONATHAN
> Daddy . . . When are we going to visit Peter?

INT. MIKE'S OFFICE

> MIKE
> That requires a little coordination. . . . Listen, I'm a
> little busy. I'll see you this weekend.

INT. JONATHAN'S BEDROOM

Discouraged, Jonathan enters to escape Danny. He takes a
puzzle out of a hiding place under the bed.

INT. MIKE'S OFFICE—DAY

Mike is working at his computer when he looks at a framed
picture of his boys.

PICTURE

BACK TO SCENE

Mike thinks a moment and suddenly punches an intercom.

> MIKE
>
> Paul . . . Mike. Do you think we're ready to lobby
> Senator Wayne? . . . I'll prepare a statement and a
> briefing package. . . . I'll call the White House.
> Maybe I can do both the same day. . . . Good. I'll try
> them now.

EXT. CENTRAL PARK WEST

FOLLOW SHOT of taxi with Mike

EXT. JONATHAN'S BLDG.

SHOT OF CAB PULLING UP

> MIKE (VO)
>
> Linda . . . Mike. I'll be coming down to D.C. next
> Wednesday, and I could bring Jonathan if you could
> watch him.

> LINDA (VO)
>
> Where should I meet you?

> MIKE (VO)
>
> Why not the Capitol steps at 10:30? Northeast
> corner.

> LINDA (VO)
>
> We'll be there. And then I have to do Meals on
> Wheels. Jonathan can help.

> MIKE (VO)
>
> Good deal.

The cab stops at the curb. Jonathan is waiting. Mike opens cab door for him. Jonathan gets in.

SHOT FROM TOP OF OUTSIDE STEPS

Danny appears in fgd.

> DANNY
>
> Daddy!

> MIKE
> (unrolling window)
>
> What, son?

> DANNY
> (holding wheel in frame)
>
> The wheel came off. Can you fix it?

Mike reluctantly gets out of the cab.

> MIKE
> (to Cabbie)
>
> I'll just be a minute.

He climbs the stairs, takes out his Swiss Army knife. He hands his briefcase to Danny.

> MIKE
>
> Hold this a sec.

Danny puts the briefcase on the stoop.

MIKE

He finishes putting on the wheel, folds his Swiss Army knife, and dashes for the cab which takes off. CAMERA PANS BACK to Mike's briefcase.

EXT. TRIBOROUGH BRIDGE

Mike's cab gets in line to get onto the Triborough.

INT. CAB

MIKE (VO)

My briefcase!

The cab makes a U-turn. Cab goes out of frame.

EXT. JONATHAN'S BLDG.

Mike's cab pulls up. Doorman rushes down the stairs, hands
Mike his briefcase. Cab moves out of frame.

EXT. MARINE AIR TERMINAL—DAY

Cab pulls up.

INT. TERMINAL

Mike and Jonathan rush in and then slow down.

WHAT THEY SEE

The terminal is empty.

INT. TICKET COUNTER

Mike buys tickets. He and Jonathan exit frame. CAMERA
PUSHES IN to clock. 10:10.

INT. WAITING ROOM

Mike is on cellular phone.

MIKE

Senator Wayne's office. . . . Uh, this is Mike Alt-

man. I'd like to get a message to the Senator that
we'll be an hour late. We had . . . uh, trouble with a
vehicle.

He dials another number.

EXT. CAPITOL STEPS—DAY

Linda and Peter enter frame, look around, and sit down on
the steps.

>   MIKE (VO)
> Linda, this is Mike. We're going to be an hour late.
> If you get this message, be sure to wait for me.
> Otherwise, I'll be stuck with Jonathan at the Senate
> and the White House.

INT. AIRPORT LOBBY

MIKE AND JONATHAN

Seated on bench.

>   JONATHAN
> When we get in, it will be 12:00. When do we get
> to the Capitol?

>   MIKE
> We should be at the Capitol at 12:30, when the
> little hand's on twelve and the big hand's on six.

>   JONATHAN
> Then you go to the White House when the little
> hand is on . . .

>   MIKE
> One . . . and the big hand on six.

He shakes his head. How could this be happening to him?

DISSOLVE

INT. AIRPORT WAITING AREA—LATER

The lobby is full.

> ANNOUNCER (VO)
> US Air announces the departure of the 11:00 shuttle to Washington, D.C.

Everyone lines up.

EXT. AIRPORT RUNWAY

Plane takes off.

EXT. CAPITOL STEPS

Linda looks at her watch.

> LINDA
> (to Peter)
> I have to deliver those Meals on Wheels.

EXT. D.C. AIRPORT RUNWAY

Plane lands.

EXT. CAPITOL STEPS

Linda and Peter go out of frame.

EXT. NATIONAL AIRPORT

Mike and Jonathan enter a cab and go out of frame.

EXT. CAPITOL STEPS

Cab arrives, CAMERA TILTS UP to Capitol dome.

Mike and Jonathan arrive and look at the area where Linda and Peter were standing before.

WHERE THEY WERE STANDING

Empty.

BACK TO SCENE

A worried Mike lectures Jonathan. Two profiles against steps.

> MIKE
> Now I don't want any babyish behavior from you.
> These are very important men that I'm going to be
> with. They make all the laws in this country, and
> they are too busy for any misbehavior. Okay?

JONATHAN

Chastised, worried. Manages to nod his head.

PROFILE ANGLE

Mike hurries up the stairs to the top.

CLOSER ON MIKE

He turns around looking for Jonathan.

JONATHAN

He is at bottom of stairs.

PROFILE ANGLE

Mike races back down the stairs.

BOTTOM OF STAIRS

Mike bends down. He is panting.

> MIKE
>
> What's wrong?

> JONATHAN
>
> Carry me.

> MIKE
>
> Carry you? Why?

> JONATHAN
>
> I'm afraid the men won't like me.

Mike, looking martyred, hands his briefcase to Jonathan, picks him up, and faces the steps again, taking them two at a time.

TOP OF STAIRS

Mike passes CAMERA, panting loudly.

INT. OLD SENATE OFFICE BLDG.

STAIRS

Mike pauses at the bottom, panting. He looks resentful. Jonathan looks scared.

TOP OF STAIRS

Mike arrives, panting more. His eyes want to close.

LANDING

A meeting has just broken up. Senators, witnesses pass CAMERA and, finally, SENATOR WAYNE. CAMERA FOLLOWS HIM. He has a word or two for about four to five people as he walks with a very sunny attitude. Suddenly he looks off, stops, and sees . . .

STAIRS

Mike, carrying Jonathan, coming up stairs. Mike is on the verge of collapse, more winded than before. Senator walks up to them. His chauffeur can be seen on the edge of the frame.

SENATOR

Hi, Mike. I heard you had car trouble.
(Mike is speechless)
Can you come back this afternoon and give us your position statement? We're all eager to be lobbied.
(Mike nods, panting)
What time can you do it?

MIKE

Unable to speak.

SENATOR

Looks to Jonathan.

JONATHAN

Rising to the occasion.

JONATHAN

He has to be at the White House at one o'clock.

SENATOR
And how long are you going to be there?

MIKE

Tries to answer, but it is hopeless.

JONATHAN

JONATHAN
Two hours.

His lips move as he computes.

JONATHAN (CONTD)
He could be back here when the little hand is on
four and the big hand is on twelve.

OVERALL SCENE

SENATOR
If you'd like the use of my car, I won't be using Jack
this afternoon.

Mike nods. JACK, a burly Irishman, steps forward. Senator
heads for the stairs. His secretary approaches him.

SECRETARY
Senator, what time will you be back?

SENATOR
(poker faced)
When the little hand's on two and the big hand's
on six.

He smiles and heads down the stairs.

SECRETARY

Amused.

MIKE

Panting.

JONATHAN

Proud.

EXT. SENATE OFFICE BLDG.—DAY

Jack holds the door open while Jonathan and Mike get into the limo. MUSIC.

EXT. BASIN DAY

The limo glides through a picturesque Washington scene.

EXT. WHITE HOUSE

The limo pulls up. Mike gets out.

INT. LIMO

Mike, Jonathan, and Jack are in the front seat, seen from the rear of seat.

CLOSER SHOT

Mike hands Jack a card.

MIKE
This is her number and her address. God knows where she is.

                              JACK
     I'll do my best.

CU JACK

Looks at card.

                              JACK
     Oh, I know Linnean Street. My old neighborhood.

EXT. WHITE HOUSE

Mike steps out of parked limo, which drives out of frame.

EXT. D.C. NEIGHBORHOODS

Limo cruises.

EXT. NEIGHBORHOOD BAR

Limo parks.

INT. LIMO

Jack gets out. Jonathan takes card with Linda's address and
phone number from the dashboard and hands it to Jack.

EXT. STREET

They walk toward the bar.

INT. BAR

BARTENDER waves.

                         BARTENDER
     Jack! Long time no see.

Jack and Jonathan walk into shot.

                              JACK
    Nice to be back.

Jack goes over to phone at corner of the bar, looks at card
with Linda's number. He dials the number, then puts down
the phone.

                              JACK
    Line's busy.

JACK'S TABLE

This table, by the window, has a view of the limo. The two
sit down.

                            WAITRESS
    Hi, Jack. How you doing? Marty's always asking
    me if I seen you. I sez no, Jack's dropped us. He's
    moving up.

Jack shakes his head.

                            WAITRESS
    That's great. What are you guys having?

                            JONATHAN
    Peanut butter and jelly.

                            WAITRESS
                            (thrown)
    Uh, I can handle that.

                              JACK
    I'll have a ham on rye and two Cokes.

Waitress goes off. MARTY enters, holding a glass of beer.

MARTY

Hey, Jack! What a sight for sore eyes.

JACK

Marty, how you doing? . . . This is Jonathan, my
friend from New York.

MARTY

Here's to you, Jonathan.

He raises his glass and sips. Jonathan raises a glass of water
and clinks Marty's glass. Then he takes the card with Linda's
name and address from Jack and goes over to the phone.

MARTY (CONTD)

What you drinking?

JACK

I got diabetes. Can't have booze.

MARTY

What are you talking about? My brother-in-law's
got diabetes and he has an occasional drink. You
want the name of his doctor?

TOWARD BAR

Jonathan's head rises into frame as he climbs on a bar stool
and dials Linda's number.

EXT. LINDA'S HOUSE—DAY

Linda answers her phone in the backyard by the pool.

LINDA

Hello . . . oh, hi, Jonathan. I wondered what happened. I just had to do Meals on Wheels for an hour.

INT. BAR

> LINDA (VO)
> I was expecting you. I pulled Peter out of play group today. (VOICE FADES) I was talking to another cousin—Selma. Remember her?

In BGD., WE HEAR

> MARTY'S VOICE (VO)
> Hey, Miss. Couple o' beers.

> JONATHAN
> We'll be there right after we eat lunch.

He sets down phone and exits frame.

EXT. STREET

POSITION CAMERA at Jack's table, looking out window to FOCUS ON Jonathan slamming his car door and then Jack slamming his. The limo drives off. CAMERA RACKS FOCUS AND TILTS DOWN to show the leavings of their sandwiches, the tip, and four empty bottles of beer.

EXT. WASHINGTON STREET

Limo travels in D.C. suburban neighborhood.

> JONATHAN
> We're going the wrong way. We were here before.

INT. LIMO

JACK AND JONATHAN

Jack's eyes are beginning to close.

JONATHAN

We have to go back!

Jack swerves left, trying to make a U-turn. Cars in the other lane SCREECH to a halt. He makes a right.

JACK

His eyes close. He steers left, not intending to do so.

EXT. STREET—DAY

Jack steers the limo into oncoming traffic in the other lane.

BICYCLER

The limo is going straight for him. The Bicycler rides into a parked car and jumps off the bike onto the hood.

PARKED D.C. POLICE CAR

The light flashes, and the SIREN TURNS ON.

JACK AND JONATHAN

Jonathan climbs onto Jack's lap, steers right, and almost hits cars that have moved from the oncoming lane into the limo's lane. One car heads toward a parked car.

CU

The car hitting the parked car.

JACK AND JONATHAN

Jonathan is sitting on Jack's lap, barely steering away from the accident and then going back to his lane.

CLOSE ON JONATHAN

His eyes widen.

WHAT HE SEES

A cross street ahead with traffic moving in both directions. ZOOM IN to cars

JONATHAN'S FEET

Trying to reach the brake pedal.

CLOSE ON JONATHAN—THROUGH WINDSHIELD

His face slides downward.

THE STREET

The limo is going to plow right into traffic.

JONATHAN'S FEET

Both feet hit the brake.

THE STREET

Pedestrians scramble. UPS man jumps out of the way of limo just as it stops. Packages spill. Miraculously, the limo stops. BRAKES SQUEAL.

OVERALL SHOT

Police car pulls behind limo. D.C. COP goes to the limo window.

WHAT HE SEES

Jonathan emerging from underneath the dashboard. He puts the limo in "park." LIGHTING EFFECT: Light rotates on Jonathan.

D.C. COP

We can see him but not hear him say "Holy shit."

INT. POLICE CAR

Jonathan holds the card with Linda's address and phone number. The Cop gets in, takes the card from Jonathan. An ambulance pulls away ahead of them.

> COP
>
> Linnean Street. Let me see.

> JONATHAN
>
> It's back that way to the right. In the three-syllable streets.

COP

His eyes widen.

> COP
>
> You drive a D.C. cab?

> JONATHAN
>
> It's my first day in Washington.

Cop pulls away.

EXT. LINDA'S HOUSE

Police car pulls into driveway. Jonathan comes around to driver's side. Linda and Peter come out of the house.

> COP
>
> You know how many lives you saved out there?

JONATHAN

How many?

COP

Two or three. Enough to make you an auxiliary member of the D.C. Police. You did some quick thinking. We can use that in the auxiliary.

JONATHAN

All smiles.

COP

He reaches into glove compartment.

JONATHAN

Cop pins the badge on him. Linda and Peter admire badge.

COP (VO)

He was quite a hero out there today.

The Cop salutes Jonathan, who returns the salute.

JONATHAN AND COUSINS

MUSIC UP as car pulls out and Jonathan starts to pantomime what he did while steering the car.

EXT. NATIONAL AIRPORT—LATE DAY

The limo speeds along, makes a turn.

EXT. NATIONAL AIRPORT

Limo pulls up. PAN TO National tower.

CLOSE ON FRONT-SEAT DRIVER

Jonathan and Mike come around to shake hands with the driver, who is the Senator.

> SENATOR
> Jonathan, when you're a little older, if you want to be a page in the Senate, you just let me know. You'd make a good one. That's the way I started.

JONATHAN

Smiling.

MIKE

Beaming.

BACK TO SCENE

Senator drives limo past them. Jonathan and Mike cross toward entrance.

EXT. SKY—LATE DAY

Plane soars in the sky.

EXT. AIRPORT RUNWAY

Plane lands.

INT. CAB, NYC

Jonathan is falling asleep in his father's arms. The thumb goes into the mouth. An old habit. Then he takes it out and wipes it on his sleeve. In a second, he falls into slumber.

EXT. JONATHAN'S BLDG.—DUSK

Taxi pulls up. Danny pedals his car over to Mike, who has the cab waiting for him.

> DANNY

Hi, Dad.

> MIKE

Hi, Danny.

Danny goes over to look at Jonathan's badge.

> DANNY

Can I wear it?

> JONATHAN

No.

> DANNY

I'll trade you the car.

> JONATHAN

Uh uh. The car is a toy. The badge is real. I'm a real auxiliary cop.

Danny gets back in the car and makes a MOTOR NOISE as he drives out of frame. Jonathan approaches the building, shows his badge to the Doorman, who salutes. He opens the door for Jonathan, who is kissed by his Mother. She has been watching Danny just inside the glass door. Jonathan shows her the badge.

THE END

10

███████████████

Launching Production

THE SCRIPT IS WRITTEN, TESTED, AND REWRITTEN. In the chapters ahead, I'll be discussing casting and working with cast, crew, and editor. But first, let's take a look at the financial considerations.

The most important question is, how will you finance your short? Most student or amateur films are funded by the filmmaker's family or by Uncle Sam in the form of a student loan, plus personal savings. There are some film grants available, but foundations take months to process applications and you may not be able to wait to see whether you are one of the lucky few. If you have "investors" who think enough of you to put in some money, that's great. Just don't tell them they will *make* money because only rarely does this happen. They may make *some* of their money back and may get a tax deduction as a capital loss if you do the proper paperwork. Keep track of your correspondence so that you can prove to the IRS that you made reasonable efforts to market the film. Even if you do make some money back, it will take years to recoup your capital and harvest profits. Investors should be able to write off their investment in a year or two, but ask an accountant for the final word.

If you are entering the film field, your short can become your calling card. It can demonstrate that you have a grasp of film, organizational ability, a talent to stir an audience with suspense, menace, humor, or whatever you do best. If you are an amateur who hopes to enter a festival and win a certificate or even a prize, so that you can travel, meet people, bask in recognition, plan your next film, then you are embarking on a potentially expensive hobby. But it need not cost a lot of money to make a short. The following tips will help you spend your money wisely, save time and money during production, and increase your chances of recouping costs.

Concentrate Locations

Design your film so most of it takes place in a compact area, one where your cast can ideally walk or bike to locations and return to home base for meals, costume changes, and phone calls. The time you save on moving from one location to another will result in more takes without interruption of your concentrated teamwork. Writer-director Danny Leiner said in an interview with my researcher and wife, Denny, that when he shot *Time Expired*, he and the cast all stayed in a borrowed house for six days. They used it for sleeping and cooking meals and also for maybe a third of the film's scenes. The other locations were within a block or two of the house. The concentration of activity and shooting paid off. This fine and funny film won the Aspen Festival's top honor for shorts, automatically placing it in nomination for a Student Academy Award.

If you can move efficiently from one location to another, your cast and crew develop a momentum, which can be destroyed by too many interruptive moves. Speed helps morale, which helps the film. Another factor in speed is adequate rehearsals that give the actors security in what they are doing. If the cast is well-rehearsed, production time will not be spent discussing what has already been settled. Experienced production people can keep up the pace of production by anticipating problems.

Another suggestion: Give gifts rather than money for the use of someone's home as a location. You could even pick something you already own—a book, an art print, and so forth, rather than a costly gift. If you have to pay a fee, then you owe nothing further than an intact home, completely cleaned, when you're finished.

Use Nonunion Actors

Actors as a rule are not paid to do a student short—even if they belong to the Screen Actors Guild (SAG). No payments are due SAG actors if the film gets shown in class or at a festival. But full union salaries plus 12.5 percent for pension and welfare *are* due if the film goes into professional TV distribution. You will end up owing your cast $445 per person times the number of shooting days, plus overtime. You could sell your short to Channel 4 in England for $7,500 (less a distribution fee of about 50 percent) and begin to face the $10,000 debt to your SAG actors. SAG actors share a percentage of producer's profits only after the distributor is paid. *But* if your cast is nonunion, you will owe them nothing, except perhaps a videotape of the final product. Remember your goal: recoup and apply all that you learned toward making another short. Do not be afraid of using nonunion actors, particularly young ones, if they are willing to rehearse with you until you like their performance. Many such players are well-trained professionals who have not yet joined SAG.

There is one additional reason not to hire SAG actors. If they are recognized as trained performers, by using them you receive less credit as director than you would if you discovered and coached unknowns or if a nonprofessional brings off a stellar performance. Bear in mind, however, that if four out of five cast members give fresh and convincing performances but the fifth person is wooden, your whole directorial contribution is open to question. It is better to replace someone who is not measuring up to the rest of the cast. More about dealing with actors in the next chapter.

Avoid Crowd Scenes

Try to avoid crowd scenes unless you are "stealing" them, that is, shooting a crowd without obtaining signed release forms, which grant permission to be filmed and acknowledge "legal consideration." (A sample release form is included in chapter 14.)

Shoot Outdoors

God is the best set designer and the most powerful gaffer. Shooting outdoors in the right place can give you a very expensive look for no money. But lighting scenes outside can sometimes be time-consuming. Also, you need to plan cover sets in case the weather turns foul. I recently saw *On the Lake*, a first-rate short by Jeremy Arnold, a Wesleyan film major, who shot a magnificent-looking coming-of-age short on Lake Placid during the summer before his senior year. It was well shot in terms of composition and coverage. It does not disparage Jeremy's work to say that he owes a lot to the weather and scenery of Lake Placid. This is not to say that one does not use lights or reflectors outdoors, but shooting without them is easier and faster. The savings in time converts to more camera setups per day and in turn, more editing choices and a better film.

The Video Option

You save raw stock costs and lab fees if you shoot on video. Afterward, you can get your finished video production transferred to film so that it will be eligible to play in festivals. Nowadays, most people whom you are trying to reach with evidence of your talent are going to want to see a cassette of your film to play at home or in the office. When you consider that your lab costs will be 40 to 50 percent of your total production costs, you should give the video option serious consideration. Many people train with professors who revere film and regret the deterioration of the image when transferred to video, and although I think all students should go through the experience of dealing with labs and film cutting, it need not be on their initial efforts. By making one or two preliminary shorts in video, students or beginners can save their money for their one relatively costly film which can be the basis for their introduction to the industry.

Shoot on Weekends

Most equipment rental houses charge you on a weekly or daily basis but not for weekends. So if you rent equipment on Friday, you can shoot three days but be charged for one when you return it Monday. Many film schools have the same policy for their equipment.

Recouping Costs

Some people are content to aim for the festival market and are not interested in TV sales. But if you are going to try to get your money back, listen to the advice of people who have been fighting to sell short films to TV. What positions your short for earning money is its appeal to European TV, where the opportunities to sell it are much better than in America. Nancy Wolzog, head of distribution at New York's Tapestry Films, says that for a short to make it in the European market, it has to be very artistic. To make it in the American market, it has to be warm, domestic, amusing, and TV length (twenty-four minutes).

Her example of a serious, artistic film is *That Burning Question*, mentioned earlier. This film was sold in fifteen countries for a total of $30,000, half of which came from the BBC. The film she cites that represents the other side of the coin, a lightweight, family film, is *The Dog Ate It*, also mentioned earlier. This film has the gentle, reassuring family values that she thinks can sell here. HBO or Showtime would pay about $8,000 for the rights to a short, half of which would go to the filmmaker. USA Network, with whom I just made a deal, pays $3,000 for one run. Bear in mind that making these sales takes years.

Wolzog says films that fall in between the two extremes of artistic and homespun do not work—that is, she cannot market them. This is not to say that she discourages filmmakers from exploring their own styles or expressing their own experiences or personal visions. In fact, she says that the best shorts come from the personal experience of the filmmaker—they have the ring of truth. She is simply saying that such films may earn no money. My own feeling is that when you leave film school you should have one short, preferably shot on tape, that reflects your personal style and one like *The Dog Ate It* that hopefully will sell to TV *and* get you a job in mainstream TV.

Stills Are Important

Nancy Wolzog urges filmmakers to have stills made of a number of scenes for distributors to use in catalogs and promotion pieces. Stills are always the last thing on your mind when you are shooting. It is disruptive and time-consuming when the still photographer comes in after the scene is shot, keeping the crew from breaking down the set and the cast from changing costumes. But your promotional pieces will be greatly enhanced by photographs.

Parlaying the Short

Employability in the industry comes from demonstrating with your short that your taste is fresh but not too elite. If drama is your forte, try to make a film teeming with viewer interest, with progressive complications, reversals, and logical surprises.

If your bent is comedy, on the other hand, don't try to make a sitcom similar to those you see on the air. The TV sitcom is a dialogue-dependent form that fills in every spare second with jokes written by a team of writers. But scratch a sitcom producer and you will find someone who really relishes fresh material— genuine comedy that comes from exposing the truth about human nature. If someone in a position to hire you sees a fresh, honest attitude in your work, he or she will assume that you are levelheaded enough to learn the constraints of the series form and perhaps to help them produce the show.

11

Working with the Actors

THE DIRECTOR'S JOB is to tell the story through the actors. This is not to diminish all the other aspects of production—camera, crew, equipment, logistics, locations, editing, and so on. But the fact is that a bad performance, perfectly lit and focused, preserved by a perfect dolly shot, will not help the film. Making a quality film begins with finding the right actors.

Casting

There are two basic styles of casting, with many shades of gray in between. The first is *typecasting*, also called on-the-nose, where the actor in the role of the football player is square-jawed and the one playing the villain looks beady-eyed and mean-spirited. The other style—*casting against type*—acknowledges that professors do not always look bookish, valedictorians do not always look nerdish, and cops are not always male, grim, and stolid. Against-type actors give an unexpected reality, a noncommercial look. But whichever style you use, the first step is to do a breakdown of all the characters you want to cast.

Character Breakdown

Here is the character breakdown for a film called *Aphrodite*, which I cowrote with the Greek writer Dimitris Nollas. You will meet up with these characters again later in the chapter.

Aphrodite: Around thirty, speaks with Greek accent. A widow in rural Greece, she has been confined to the family dairy farm, under her father's thumb, heeding the Greek custom that a widow cannot appear in mixed company, let alone date or marry. She is obedient on the surface but smolders with frustration.

Monica: Mid-thirties. An American living in Athens, she is forthright, outspoken, an independent member of a generation that has torn up all the old rules that confine Aphrodite. Because of her age, she is worried about both her ticking biological clock and her late-starting career.

Paul: Forty. An American of Greek ancestry employed as a Balkan correspondent for a TV news service. Outrageously sentimental, neurotically charged, at times self-doubting, and at other times pontifical, Paul obsesses over babies and dreams of finally starting a family.

Niki: Fifty, speaks with Greek accent. A sweet and accommodating Greek wife under increasing pressure to stand up to her patriarchal husband. She both arouses and then denies her husband in order to break his grip on the unhappy status quo.

Elias: Sixty, speaks with Greek accent. A bombastic domestic tyrant, he denies his widowed daughter any freedom in order to keep his reputation secure with the other villagers.

Finding Actors

Where do you find your cast? A common approach in New York City is to advertise in the newspaper *Backstage*; in Los Angeles, ads are placed in *Drama-Logue*. The ad must state whether the film is SAG or non-SAG. If you are shooting SAG, you need to go to the local office and negotiate a contract. You will also need to get the insurance specified by SAG even though you will *not* have to pay wages until the film is in distribution and is returning a profit.

If you live outside a production center, ads in college papers or in show business periodicals are the usual way of finding potential actors. You can also contact community theaters, college drama societies, and the drama and film departments at colleges and universities. (Going this route in 1962, I found Jon Voight through Catholic University.) If you are shooting with non-SAG actors, indicate that you will only be paying for expenses. Describe the type of actor you want (age, height, and other characteristics), and be sure to include a phone number. Most people who are interested will want to check you out to assure themselves that the project is legitimate.

Auditions

Find a place big enough to provide an auditioning room and a separate reception area. Appoint someone to receive the actors, sign them in, and give them a copy of the script. On the script cover, indicate the pages the actors should read over before they audition, and include a one-page summary of the story. The person acting as a receptionist should bring in and introduce each candidate in turn. You also should have on hand a couple of people who will read well with the actors. Choose audition scenes that bring out the emotional range of the role. If a character moves from being docile in the status quo to explosive later on, pick scenes that bring out these two extremes. Use a video camera—borrow one if necessary—to tape the audition so you will have a record of it, and note the footage where each candidate starts and ends so you can quickly locate the various performances. Later, if you are having trouble deciding between two actors, you can replay their segments and compare performances.

Many directors will ask the actor to drop the script and improvise the scene. Improvisation can better show you an actor's behavior than a reading of the lines. (My own policy is to ask an actor to improvise only when I think the person is right for the role.) You might request that the actor do some of the eyeplay or dawning-realization scenes so you can see the process of change. *Process* is an acting term that refers to the thinking and feeling that a character undergoes in the course of a scene. The opposite of process is *result acting*. The result that the script indicates may be rage, but a good actor shows the process of the rage building.

If you do think a candidate has potential for the role, get behind the camera and start directing him or her. Now it is *your* turn to improvise. Describe the inner thoughts of the character, giving the actor unwritten lines to think about and spontaneously respond to.

The audition can be an opportunity to test your material—to see how your dialogue is working, to change it if it isn't. It also affords the opportunity to rethink some of your casting ideas by switching actors around, trying them in different roles. During an audition, I often cut or add a sentence, change a word, or make notes to write a new scene. And sometimes, when I improvise with the actors, they come up with material that is better than the original.

Once you have decided on a cast, start bonding with your actors. Always phone them yourself to say they have the part. Be generous with praise. Tell them why you cast them, what you like about their acting. Call the near-misses as well, and keep their names, phone numbers, and head shots on file. You may have to look to a runner-up if you come to have second thoughts about an actor you've cast, if an actor has second thoughts about staying with the project, or if an actor cannot make the rehearsal or shooting schedule.

Directing the Actor

The directing method I advocate here comes from stage director Harold Clurman, who derived it from Konstantin Stanislavsky, the founder of the Moscow Art Theater. He is the man who changed modern acting by originating and passing on a process of acting that in the United States is called "The Method." Several Americans went over to Russia to study this technique, Harold Clurman and Stella Adler among them. They then passed it on to my teacher Curt Conway, another member of the Group Theater, the young and fiery theater company that enlivened Broadway in the thirties. When I studied with Conway in 1959, I used to see many of the actors who are now familiar to the public—Dustin Hoffman, Robert Duvall, Joanne Woodward, Jerome Ragni, and Barbra Streisand—as they mastered the technique. That year, Conway invited Clurman to come to class to give his famous lecture on directing. I was privileged to hear this lecture twice. Clurman was so passionate and enthusiastic that he would always end up shouting and screaming. Then he would ask the audience, *"Do you think I'm screaming now?* THIS IS MY NORMAL TONE OF VOICE!" Clurman did not have much of a film career, but stage and film director Elia Kazan embraced this method, crediting Clurman for teaching it to him. The approach is simple, but making it your own takes a long time, perhaps a lifetime. Here is "The Method."

Divide each scene into beats, that is, units in the scene that begin and end when there is a change of energy, attitude, approach, the entrance of a new character, or new information. For example, in *Beat 1* the antagonist has the protagonist tied up and is asking him to tell where the money is hidden. The man refuses. The tormenter puts a knife to the man's throat, drawing blood, but the man again refuses to talk. *Beat 2:* The door opens, and two henchmen bring in the man's son, bound and gagged. The man still insists he does not know where the money is. *Beat 3:* The door opens, and the man's daughter is brought in crying. She pleads with her eyes. The man does not relent. *Beat 4:* The captors rip her blouse with a knife. The man begins to sweat and starts to yield.

In each beat, the actor is given an action to play, expressed by the infinitive of a verb—for instance, to prove, to seduce, to overpower. The director has to decide the "how," expressed by an adverb or a gerund. Clurman said that when he directed he would reveal the verb, also called the action, but he never showed the actor his note about how a scene should be played—that is, crying or laughing or whatever. He always wrote this note in his script on the blank page opposite the text, then waited to see whether the actor would discover a "how" close to his own. The actor usually did. Giving the actor the joy of a discovery is more empowering than trying to tell the actor to do something that does not come from within.

The scene, as written, may not have obvious beats. Even the writer may not be aware of them. The director *imposes* his or her own action script upon the text and invents a sequence of beats that reveals the inner emotional progression of the characters and becomes a blueprint for the actors. If you are going to direct your own material, you still must try to rediscover your scene and break it down into beats. Actors and directors refer to the dialogue as the text—only one element of the scene. When you switch hats from writer to director, you should share the actor's vision of the scene instead of trying to protect the text in a literal way.

To enrich the scene, the director also writes the subtext for each beat and asks the actor to interpolate it. Frequently, in a man-woman scene, for example, two opposed characters play the text as a love scene even though that love will never be consummated. I can recall a cop-murderer interrogation scene in *The Onion Fields*, directed and played as a seduction scene.

As the director, you create the beats so that the action can rise and the drama progress in each successive beat. Give each beat a name that takes the form of a short sentence—Ron begs for a job; Maude gets high; Herb crashes. Then write in the margin or on the back of the previous page how the action should be played. When writing your sentences, use active verbs to give the actors (1) something to do and (2) somewhere to build to emotionally.

Let us look at Beat 1 of the above example. The captured man might take one of the following actions. Choose one.

ACTION	HOW
to refuse	defiantly
to deny	vehemently
to protest	innocently
to insist	forcefully
to convince	overpoweringly

I choose "to protest innocently" because it leaves the actor somewhere to go. It gives the tormentor something to do—to scorn his innocence—menacingly. When the son is brought in, the man's action could be to insist forcefully. When his daughter is brought in, his action could become "to bargain," rather than "to plead," which is somewhat weaker.

Often a subtext exists that undercuts the literal words of the text. Playing the subtext allows for ambivalence—the comingling of two often contradictory emotions: A widow can grieve for her husband and relish her new freedom. Such duality is true to human nature and often enhances the actor's performance. If actors do not take the text literally as one-dimensional, they can expand the scope of the scene and surprise the audience. The problem for actors is that when the subtext is added, it often becomes the dominant color of the scene rather than the highlight. Rehearsals are the place to find the balance between the text and the subtext. When a scene has a strong subtext, that subtext becomes the action of the beat. Usually, a director does not give two actions.

I have selected a few pages from the previously mentioned film *Aphrodite* to give you a more detailed example of how to break the text down into beats and actions. Note that a new camera setup always signals a new beat. After reading over the scenes that follow, test yourself by giving each beat a name; give the actors an action to play, and write in the "hows." The beats are numbered so that you can turn to the end of this section to find the names and the actions I have assigned.

BEAT 1
EXT. CONSTITUTION SQUARE—ATHENS, GREECE—
EVENING

PAN TO AN APARTMENT HOUSE NEAR THE

SQUARE. MONICA, an attractive, athletic Californian with a punk hairdo, mid-30s, gets out of a van marked TVN Productions in English and in Greek, and walks into her apartment building. She can be seen ringing for the elevator.

INT. HALLWAY OF APARTMENTS 7–9

Monica emerges from the elevator, walks down the hall to apartment 7, puts her sound recording gear inside, runs past apartment 8 to apartment 9, knocks urgently on the door. PAUL, around 40, also American, answers. She throws her arms around him. They kiss passionately.

BEAT 2

> MONICA
>
> Darling, I tried desperately to reach you. There were no phones near the shoot. Did you feel abandoned?

> PAUL
>
> Totally. I thought you'd met some cameraman or something.

> MONICA
>
> I missed you every second.

> PAUL
>
> Prove it.

She pulls her T-shirt off, throws it into his apartment. Paul lifts her off her feet as they kiss, backs into his apartment, and closes the door.

BEAT 3

With hardly a pause, WE CUT TO Monica some time later, wearing Paul's towel, leaving his apartment, carrying her clothes. He gives her a final kiss.

> PAUL
> What do you want for breakfast?

> MONICA
> Waffles . . . sleep well.

> PAUL
> Night, love.

BEAT 4

In sequence, they each bang their doors closed. PAUSE. She opens her door, and half a beat later, Paul opens his door and brings the book she forgot. She takes it from him and closes the door. A lady in her late 50s emerges from apartment 8, putting on her robe. She marches to apartment 9, Paul's, knocks loudly. Paul answers.

> PAUL
> Oh, Mrs. Goulandris, were we making too much noise?

> MRS. GOULANDRIS
> This opening-closing all hours of the night. It's endless. Why don't you and I trade apartments? You can break through and I'll have the corner view.

> PAUL
> Mrs. Goulandris, you're brilliant.

She shuts her door. Monica opens her door, brushing her teeth.

> PAUL
>
> Honey . . .

> MONICA
>
> It's too soon.

> PAUL
>
> Two and a half years?

> MONICA
>
> Don't push, love. Night.

She closes her door. Chastised, Paul walks toward his door.

BEAT 5

EXT. TOWN SQUARE—MONOKLISSIA, GREECE—DAY

A wedding couple emerges from the church. A band of musicians plays as friends and relatives, laughing and throwing rice, accompany them to the festooned car. A TITLE READS: "Monoklissia, Greece. Population: 498." TITLES CONTINUE.

APHRODITE AND THE OLDER WIDOWS

Watching from a distance, excluded.

THE CHURCH

The bride and groom get into a car as people throw flower petals. Before they drive off, the father of the groom, AN-

DREAS, approaches his son. ANDREAS is dressed in naval whites.

> ANDREAS
> (sotto voce)
> Don't drive past the widows. Bad luck.

WIDOW BENCH

Most of the adults in Monoklissia are at the wedding. Only the Widows sit apart, all in black, sewing and embroidering dance costumes. Among them sits beautiful APHRODITE, out of place among the old gossips.

CLOSE ON APHRODITE

Her eyes are riveted on the wedding party. She is sad and isolated.

TOWN SQUARE

The Groom drives toward the Widows, then makes a U-turn, and drives off in the other direction. TITLES END.

APHRODITE

Feeling the slight, she gets up and walks in the direction of the car.

> WIDOW
> Aphrodite, where you going this time?

> APHRODITE
> To get a newspaper.

> SECOND WIDOW
> The costumes won't sew themselves.

THIRD WIDOW
Women's Day is coming—ready or not.

They laugh, covering their toothless mouths.

APHRODITE

Walking away, picks up a flower that fell from the wedding car.

BEAT 6

EXT. GRAVEYARD—DAY

Aphrodite holds the flower as she lights a candle and picks at some crabgrass encroaching on the headstone.

APHRODITE (VO)
Stavros, remember the good times we used to have in Serres? What's the harm if I took a job there—just to see something beside widows and cows?

EXT. A BUS STOP ON THE WAY TO SERRES

Aphrodite buys a newspaper at the kiosk, immediately turns to the want ads, then steps out of frame as a bus arrives.

HER FANTASY

Her husband has his arm around her as they move toward the bus. She is wearing pink.

BEAT 7

ANOTHER ANGLE—REALITY

Now dressed in black, she approaches the bus until YIANNIS, a gossip, sees her.

> YIANNIS
>
> Going to Serres, Aphrodite?

She snaps out of her daze.

> APHRODITE
>
> No.

She watches him get on, and the bus pulls off without her.

BEAT 8

EXT. ANDREAS'S DAIRY FARM

ELIAS, Aphrodite's bombastic father, 60, and her sweet and serene mother, NIKI, 50, take their leave from the bridal party. The social smile fades quickly on the face of the smoldering Elias as he puts his 5-year-old grandson, Menelaos, on his shoulders.

> ELIAS
>
> That stupid Andreas . . .

> NIKI
>
> Elias . . . he's your cousin.

> ELIAS
>
> Having the nerve to wear a white uniform. At his height—the pinnacle of his career—he was a cabin boy.

They walk across the common meadow toward their own

dairy farm. In the distance, Aphrodite herds cows absent-mindedly while reading the newspaper.

BEAT 9

CLOSER ON APHRODITE

Herding cows inattentively as she studies the want ads in the newspaper. She circles an ad.

ELIAS—WALKING CLOSER

Seeing something he dislikes, he shouts to his daughter.

> ELIAS
>
> Aphrodite, you have one of Andreas's cows. Where is your head?

> APRHODITE
>
> Sorry, Papa.

APHRODITE

She finds the errant cow and leads it toward her father.

ELIAS

Walking toward her.

> ELIAS
>
> Remember when this happened before? Andreas never shut up.

He runs to help her expel the stray cow, expressing toward it the venom he feels for his cousin, Andreas.

BEAT 10

THE COWSHED—MOMENTS LATER

Her eyes still on the ads in the paper, Aphrodite milks the cows and talks to her mother.

> APHRODITE
> Mama, I have to go to Serres this week.

> NIKI
> For feed?

> APHRODITE
> A job interview.

> NIKI
> Your father will not permit it.

> APHRODITE
> Can't you talk to him?

> NIKI
> I'll try. But he always says "too soon."

BEAT 11

EXT. CAFÉ—LATE DAY

Elias sits playing backgammon. Andreas enters in his wedding costume. He is a portly man with military bearing and a florid face, the same age as Elias. Men offer their hands in congratulations.

> MEN
> Hey, Andreas. Congratulations. Quite a wedding.

Heard the music. Lot of presents. Your son did okay.
Nice boy.

Andreas makes a sweep of the café, ends up with his back to
Elias.

> ELIAS
>
> So. Where are they going to live—the couple?

> ANDREAS
>
> With us. You'll have two new neighbors. Maybe
> three.

He winks. Laughter ripples around the table.

> ELIAS
>
> How you going to feed another family with just a
> few cows?

Andreas smiles ominously.

> ANDREAS
>
> We have a plan.

Andreas walks away. Elias's backgammon Partner leans in to
whisper.

> PARTNER
>
> They say the girl brings a big dowry.

Elias sniffs at this information.

> ELIAS
>
> I still have the largest herd in this part of Mace-
> donia.

Within earshot, Andreas turns around, smiling. Elias picks up the backgammon dice, blows on them, and rolls.

> ELIAS (CONTD)
> Come on, babies. I need double sixes.

As the dice land, he punches the air with excitement, moves his pieces. Andreas looks at Elias, relishing the misery he has in store for him.

BEAT 12

INT. APHRODITE'S ROOM—DAWN

Aphrodite lies asleep with a man's hand resting on her breast. Suddenly the reality of a HORN BLAST intrudes. She is startled awake.

ANOTHER ANGLE

The hand is gone. THE HORN CONTINUES.

BEAT 13

EXT. ROAD IN FRONT OF ELIAS'S HOUSE—DAWN

In fgd., Andreas is BLASTING THE HORN of Elias's truck that is badly parked and blocking the narrow road. In bgd. are two large trucks filled with Andreas's "secret plan." The plan consists of ten additional white cows. Elias, summoned in his pajamas, approaches in shoes without socks.

> ELIAS
> Where did all these cows come from?

ANDREAS

It's my daughter-in-law's dowry.

Elias insults him as he reparks.

ELIAS

What kind of wedding present is a herd of cows?
You people never heard of furniture?

In the distance, another truck with another six cows is about
to follow.

ELIAS (CONTD)

Silverware? . . . Dishes?

By now Elias has reparked his truck. He calls out to Andreas, who is passing him in the first of the two trucks filled
with cows.

ELIAS

Where are you going to feed them?

ANDREAS

Where I always feed my cows. In the land we got
from Uncle Dimitris.

ELIAS

You better find some other place. It's crowded
enough.

ANDREAS

You find some other place. Don't start with me.

CAMERA ON ELIAS

As Andreas drives off, he blows dust on Elias. The second

truck passes and does the same. Elias smolders: "I'll catch up with that bastard."

BEAT 14

INT. PAUL'S BEDROOM—MORNING

Darkness. The SOUNDS of postcoital nuzzling. Monica, on top, lights Paul's cigarette.

>   MONICA
> Happy birthday.

>   PAUL
> How did *you* like my present?

>   MONICA
> On a scale of one to a hundred?

>   PAUL
> Mmm-hmmm.

>   MONICA
> Ninety-nine.

>   PAUL
> We have to leave something for marriage.

She puts a finger on his lips, warns him playfully.

>   MONICA
> Don't start.

BEAT 15

INT. PAUL'S LIVING ROOM—LATER

Monica has served Paul a tray with eggs benedict, orange juice, coffee, and a muffin with a sizzling candle on top. He stares at it without appetite as she goes back to the kitchen to get another tray for herself. Paul nibbles at the edge of the muffin.

> MONICA
> (sitting)
> What's wrong, Paulie? Not hungry?

Behind Paul rests a portrait of Paul as a child with an older father.

> PAUL
> My father had me very late. He was more like a grandfather. He died when I was in high school. I never had any brothers or sisters.

Monica puts down her food.

> MONICA
> Paul, I don't need this kind of pressure.

> PAUL
> Pressure?

She sits with Paul. She is moody.

> MONICA
> To get married, have a baby.

> PAUL
> I'm sorry.

> MONICA
> You're turning into a nag.

PAUL

I haven't said a word.

MONICA

Paul, what if I can't?

PAUL

Marry?

MONICA

Conceive.

PAUL

How do you know unless you try?

MONICA

Let's just follow this out. We get married. We try.
We can't. You'll feel stuck.

PAUL

Never.

MONICA

You'll still want a baby.

PAUL

Yes . . . but I want one with *you*.

MONICA

. . . Paul, we've got a problem.

She begins to cry.

MONICA (CONTD)

For a year now . . . ever since you started on this

marriage and baby theme, I've used no birth control
. . . to see if I could . . . And . . . I never came close.
I've been consulting a doctor. . . . He doesn't think I
can get pregnant.

> PAUL
> (quietly)
> This doesn't change a thing.

> MONICA
> (getting up)
> It's a deal breaker, isn't it?

Paul does not deny it. THE PHONE RINGS. Paul answers it.

BEAT 16

> PAUL
> Kirk? Hi. . . . Yes. Sure, I can do it.
> . . . Uh, Monica? . . . Let me ask her.

> MONICA
> I'm not going on location with you.

> PAUL
> We don't have to stay together.

> MONICA
> I'm not going.

> PAUL
> (to phone)
> I don't think she can make it to Monoklissia.

MONICA

Wait a minute! *Women's Day*? In that funny town?

PAUL

Monoklissia.

MONICA

I wouldn't miss it!

PAUL

Uh . . . Kirk . . . she can make it after all. Who do you have for camera? . . . Nicholas Kamakis?

MONICA

I'm not working with him.

Paul covers the phone.

PAUL
(whispering loudly)

I can't let you veto the cameraman.

MONICA

That is the Nicholas I told you about.

Paul gets furious over the very idea of Nicholas.

PAUL
(to phone)

Uh, Kirk . . . we both have a problem with Nicholas. Is there anybody . . .

Suddenly, he hears a CLICK.

MONICA

What did he say?

PAUL

He said it's a shoot, not a dinner party.

Monica steels herself against a doubly difficult experience.
Paul clears his plate and dumps Monica's birthday breakfast
into the garbage.

Here are my notes about the beats and actions of the first few
pages of *Aphrodite*. Where the stage directions are clear about the
actors' action, I have not added any directorial notes.

Beat 1. Monica Rushes to Paul: Entering the
building, she looks at her watch while waiting for the elevator.
One might give her the action "to rush." But if you simply tell the
actress to enter and ring for the elevator, her acting will be milder
than if you tell her to hurry the elevator, in which case, she will
keep pressing the button, put her gear down and pace with her
hand still on the button.

Beat 2. Monica Atones: Monica's action is to reassure
Paul's insecurity. How: emphatically. Paul's action is to question
her loyalty. This will make him search her eyes for any telltale sign
of disloyalty. In this beat, they open the door.

Beat 3. Paul Reveals His Insecurity: In the next
beat, Paul's action is to woo her by offering to cook her breakfast.
Monica's action is to minimize her delight by acting nonchalant.

*Beat 4. Mrs. Goulandris Suggests Cohabita-
tion:* It begins when Mrs. Goulandris opens her door "to trade
apartments." Her "how" is maternally. Monica's action is to resist
marriage sweetly. Paul's action is to press marriage routinely. It is
an ongoing, everyday discussion.

*Beat 5. Aphrodite Wants to Change from
Widow to Bride World:* Her action is to escape un-

noticed. She wants to appear interested in widow activities so as not to give offense—but the subtext is that sitting on the widow's bench feels unnatural. She is not reconciled to her status.

Beat 6. Aphrodite Asks Stavros's Permission to Leave Monoklissia: Aphrodite's action is to seduce Stavros, just as she did when he was alive. In a fantasy, she imagines his protection at the bus stop.

Beat 7. Aphrodite is Caught by a Gossip: Her action is to sneak. She puts a shawl around her head. Yiannis's action is to turn her into delicious gossip. Aphrodite accepts defeat—for now.

Beat 8. Elias Berates His Cousin Andreas: Elias's action is to prosecute Andreas in a court martial where Niki—if she would just shut up and listen—is the sole judge.

Beat 9. Elias Warns Aphrodite: His action with Aphrodite is to prevent a nightmare recurrence of a time when Andreas could justly criticize him. The "how" is panic-stricken. Aphrodite's action is to feign interest, first in cattle and then in her father's demands.

Beat 10. Aphrodite Tries to Get Niki's Backing Against Elias: In the cowshed, when Aphrodite asks her mother, her action is to petition for permission to work; her "how" is desperately. The subtext is that she wants to end her widowhood. Niki's action is to forestall her lovingly.

Beat 11. Elias and Andreas Assert Superiority Over Each Other: Elias's action is to make his claim to wealth proudly. Andreas's action is to hint smugly about the new cows he is expecting.

Beat 12. Aphrodite Dreams That Stavros Still Protects Her

Beat 13. Andreas Shatters the Status Quo: Elias's action is to protect his dominance as the largest dairy farmer in the area. He does this warily, sensing a threat. Andreas's action is to threaten Elias competitively. Elias's action is to humiliate Andreas sarcastically. Andreas's action is to counterattack with pent-up exasperation.

Beat 14. Paul Presses for Marriage: In the beginning of the beat, Monica wants to preserve the status quo peacefully.

Beat 15. Monica Confesses: Paul's action in the beat, which begins with his speech about his father, is to change the conversation from standoff to a candid revelation of the problem from his perspective. Her action then is to reveal her infertility, defiantly, testing to see whether he will leave her.

Beat 16. Paul, Then Monica, Are Pulled into the Monoklissia Story: When the phone rings, Paul's action is to act professional. When Monica hears Nicholas's name, her action is to avoid working with a man she has slept with. Paul's action is to keep Monica, but the subtext is that he wants to drop her if she is definitely infertile. After he hangs up, his action is to defy Monica by quoting Kirk.

Directorial Style

A director's style can be eccentric (Jim Jarmusch), sardonic and cinematic (Alfred Hitchcock), realistic but absurd (Preston Sturges), and so forth. Style is Hitchcock's showing Cary Grant in *North by Northwest* waiting beside a road for an attacker who comes by plane instead of a car. When Ivan Passer directed his first short *Intimate Lighting*, he bewildered his crew who were ready to shoot when he refused to signal his assistant director (AD) to roll the camera: He was waiting for a butterfly—the symbol of lightness—to dance into the frame. Style is director Jack Clayton's letting you see Lawrence Harvey's smoke rings in *Room at the Top* before you meet him. What do those smoke rings mean? They hint of a man who desires a measure of control.

In every scene, the director imposes a concept, that is, an idea about the scene beyond what is indicated in the text. Often the concept ties the story to political tides of the day. If you have a teenage villain, you may want to make him a skinhead with a twisted cross of hair growing in the back of his head. Then instead of being simply someone blocking the hero, he represents a malevolent force alive in society. Once I directed a scene where two people seemed to be at odds, spelling out things that they admired without seeming to acknowledge what the other was saying. I directed this scene with the concept that it was an attempt to communicate rather than an attempt to ignore and devalue what the other person was saying.

Clurman said that, above all, the director must be interesting. He or she must mull over the script to come up with fresh actions that release the emotions and increase the tensions of the story. Actors have a name for directors who are not clear on actions and who deal only with the literal text: They call them traffic cops. Giving the actors and the camera moves is only the minimum that a director should do.

Rehearsals

The courtship of the cast, begun in auditions, continues with the beginning of rehearsals. The first rehearsal is often a reading where everyone is seated at a table to read and examine the text.

Your principal actors should be there but not your bit players. (The best time to rehearse nonprincipals is right before a take.) Let somebody else like the AD read the minor roles at this session. When the cast finishes, you should make a short statement on what the film is about, what it means to you emotionally, and what you will need from the actors to make the film come off. Talk about style can come at this time, if it comes at all. Often style cannot be put into words and is arrived at by trial and error.

This is also the time to clarify ambiguities in the text, to entertain questions, and to take up any problems that remain unsettled, such as uncast roles. If a performance seems off the mark, it is better to make some general remarks privately to the actor who displeases you. If you do not criticize privately, it looks as if you are singling out that person. This is the democratic phase of directing when you should be extremely flexible. By the end of rehearsals, the actors should have decided how they are going to play the role. When you finally go into production, everyone should know what to do—where to sit, how to behave, when to cross, and so forth. All that must be supplied is the illusion of the first time to give freshness to a rehearsed performance.

The best place to rehearse is on the sets where you will actually shoot. If you cannot do so, use a rehearsal space where you can tape the floor to give the dimensions of the real set. Rehearse your material one beat at a time. Give the actor the verb, but let him or her discover the adverb, the "how." By giving the actor an action, you prevent him or her from "playing a quality," which is very general. The more specific the acting, the better the performance.

How the actor does the action should come more from the actor than the director. Whether the action is done while the actor is crying, laughing, angry, or showing all three emotions at once, if the "how" comes from inside the actor, it will play better. You are allowing the performer to create from personal experience. Of course, you must take charge of the emotion you want the audience to feel. It is always tempting for an emotional actor to cry at a moment when you want the audience to be moved, thus violating an old acting rule: "The audience cries. You don't." Which is more moving to viewers, tears slowly forming in the eyes of someone they find empathetic, or the same actor boo-hooing uncontrollably? Avoid self-pity in your performers. It is the audience's job to grieve, the actor's job, to show the character's courage. In a comic situation, as well, the actor should not laugh. That is the audience's prerogative.

Let's watch an imagined rehearsal of the screenplay we broke into beats. It is the graveyard scene where Aphrodite tries to get her deceased husband's permission to go to town. If the actress comes in looking sad because she is a widow, pleading for permission, the performance will be very general, that is, it will have an overall wash of sadness that would be appropriate for all widows. To make it specific, I might rehearse the actress as follows: "Aphrodite, come into the graveyard. Don't be plaintive. Your action is *to seduce* your husband into giving you permission to go into town. . . . Don't whimper. Charm him. Show that he rejects you. At first, he doesn't want you to go into town. It's a setback for you. . . . Good. That twitching of the lips is good. Dead or alive, he'll never resist that. Do it again. . . . Excellent. I like the way you tidied your hair as you approached the gravestone. Nice touch."

Emotional Memory

Respect the actor's process during rehearsals. It is a rare coincidence if an actor has experienced the exact same things as the character he or she is portraying. The actor's most valuable asset is the ability to access personal feelings from an emotional memory bank and integrate them into the scene. Usually, the actor develops this repertoire of emotions by doing exercises either in acting class or privately at home. But some untrained people have an instinct for certain characters that makes them effective on film.

Sometimes the genuine emotion evoked by the actor is too strong and overwhelms the scene. In such instances the actor needs "to cover" the emotion with a layer of courage or toughness or the action "to conceal." Scenes in which the primary color of a raw emotion is muted by a cover can be very effective. In fact, lying or dissembling to other characters but revealing the true feelings to the audience makes for very good film. Think of *Passion Fish* where Alfre Woodard's character concealed her tortured past but hinted at her hurt and resentment in every line.

Usually, film directors do not collaborate with actors on emotional memory as stage directors do. That's because the film rehearsal period is short (for reasons of cost) and because the discontinuous nature of film acting focuses on getting one scene at a time correct. On the stage, the actor needs to build a performance from the ground up, and it is more appropriate for the director to share his or her secret emotional sources.

But if the performance is not coming, if it has dried up between rehearsal and shooting, it is the director's job to stimulate the actor's emotions. If I were speaking to the actress playing Aphrodite under these circumstances, the first thing I would do would be to describe the emotional experience from the character's point of view: "You miss your husband horribly. The way he made love, the way he could make you laugh at nothing . . . and the way he liked to surprise you." I would then get the actress to continue, to pick up the thread and try to recollect when a lover surprised *her*. As she talks about such a memory or silently accesses the memory, I would then switch to the scene I was shooting and roll the camera as soon as possible. It's important for both director and actor to remember why they are doing all this—to reveal emotional truth to the camera.

Illusion of the First Time

The illusion of the first time is an impression given to an audience that these words are being spoken and this behavior displayed for the first time. When an actor can surprise the audience in this way, it increases credibility, empathy, and spontaneity. Geraldine Page once summarized for me what many acting teachers have said: The character has not read the screenplay; the character does not know how the scene or the story or even the *sentence* will end.

The illusion of groping for words—of sorting out interfering words and thoughts—can be found in the work of our best actors. Jane Fonda is never so convincing as when she reveals the character's inner uncertainty in such films as *The China Syndrome*. Warren Beatty, Diane Keaton, and Woody Allen also give the impression of improvising, not spitting out unhesitatingly the words of a memorized script. Think of such films as *Reds* and *Annie Hall*. Good actors allow us to see the process—the inner workings of the character as he or she absorbs surprises, changes emotions and attitudes.

Directing the Nonprofessional

Nonprofessionals—as opposed to trained and talented actors who are either SAG or non-SAG—are usually cast because they are the right type, that is, they look like the character. But sometimes they sound as if they are reading a line instead of speaking from the heart. They have trouble memorizing lines and get more nervous every time they flub. The secret of getting a good performance from a non-pro begins with the script. Pare down their lines into very short sentences. If a line can be turned into an action, shoot the action. It will play better than the wooden reading you will get. The second rule with amateurs is to keep them active when you are staging a scene. Don't let them settle into a situation where they sit and talk for a while. If you have more than a line or two, you can get your character moving and shoot from a long shot, recording line readings leisurely after shooting to lay in during editing. Use close-ups of the actors reacting to something that is visually strong.

The technique of using the nonprofessional is derived in part from the early film experiments of Vsevolod Pudovkin, who maintained in his writings and in his films that the meaning of a shot comes from the preceding shot. To illustrate his point, he shot close-ups of a girl against a neutral background. He then showed this close-up spliced next to a shot of a puppy and asked an audience to describe the girl's emotion. They thought she looked affectionate. He then showed the same close-up after a scene of cruelty, and to the same audience she looked sad. In fact, the girl was just staring at the camera, thinking of nothing. Intercutting close-ups of your nonprofessional with shots of objects, actions, and other actors instead of trying to articulate wrenching emotions is one way to shape their performance.

Always give the nonprofessionals something to do with their hands: pet a dog, snack on fruit, use a hairbrush, lay a fire, chop wood. It is very hard for even a rank amateur to blow the scene if a dog is licking his or her face (because you have smeared it with liver). You can also count on a scene in which the nonactor is doing something that he or she does all the time. It is easy for a real-life dentist to play a dramatic scene set in a dental office or for a bartender to say lines while mixing drinks at a bar.

If a nonprofessional has an important part, avoid starting production with dialogue scenes that require acting. Start with long shots of her or him moving—walking or driving, for example. A couple of days of easy shots and socializing with the crew and cast will give the nonpro confidence. Then you can start shooting dialogue scenes, saving the hardest for last.

If you cannot avoid long speeches, simply plan cutaways to get you from one take to another. It is standard practice in Hollywood to do what are called pickups. You shoot until you get past a cutting point. If the actor flubs after that, you then pick the scene up from the point where you have a cut to a reaction shot or to a cutaway. Plan the cutting points carefully so you always know whether you can pick up or not.

In the next chapter, I will discuss the role of the crew in helping to render the director's vision.

12

Working
with the
Crew

THE FILMMAKER INFUSES his POV through the crew, who help
put concepts and style onto film. To use your time and resources
efficiently, a number of crew jobs have to be covered. These are:
cinematographer; assistant director (AD); assistant cinematographer (AC) with film, engineer with video (often the engineer also
does sound mixing); script clerk (also called dialogue director or
continuity director); gaffer; grip; sound mixer; costume designer;
prop person; and makeup person. Let's examine these disciplines
one at a time.

Cinematographer

This is the all-important person who directs the lighting of the
set, frames the scene (in collaboration with the director) from the
beginning to the "cut" point, plans and executes camera moves,
imposes a visual style, and prompts the director to make sure the
scene is covered, that is, shot from a variety of overlapping angles
to allow for editing choices.

Craft genealogy is important to me. I always feel better if I can connect my mentors with the great figures of film and literature. I am fortunate in that my first real cameraman was Guilgialmo (Bill) Garroni, who worked in Italy with the great silent-film director William Pabst as well as with Vittorio De Sica and Roberto Rossellini. Garroni taught me a great deal about these masters and about film in general. He loved lighting and was one of the first cinematographers in the United States to light sets for color film with the same modeling (play of light and shadow) as black and white. He taught me what Pabst taught him about finding the frame and then filling it. He was always telling me what De Sica would do in my position. I owe him thanks for teaching me his uncompromising approach to the image and for tolerating my youthful willfulness.

Working smoothly and creatively with the cinematographer in selecting lenses and designing camera movement is a vital part of directing. A creative partnership requires that when there is conflict, the director should concede in matters of aesthetics and the cinematographer should concede in matters of storytelling. Cinematographers tend to be assertive and argumentative until two things happen—they realize that they are being heard and heeded or they become busy with a task. In general, cinematographers fall into two categories: Some are highly technical, and others long to direct. The latter may pester you with directing ideas. If you find yourself constantly deflecting suggestions, give your cinematographer a challenging problem to worry about, such as figuring out how to mount the camera on a vehicle.

Cinematographers are extremely visual people who will usually see a scene from a new perspective. They will feel strongly about where and how to frame the shot and how to move the camera. Good ones want to avoid the cliché and head-on photography.

Often, however, they will not be tuned in to the story in the same way that you are and need to be reminded about the purpose of the shot. It will help if you have already designed your shots and can articulate the dramatic reasons for them. Another difference between you is that your mind will be darting ahead to upcoming shots that you are worried about, whereas the cinematographer will be thinking one shot at a time.

After positioning the camera and setting the movement, the cinematographer's main job is to light the set, certainly the most time-consuming of all production activities. He or she must first deal with *motivating the light*, that is, making the film light appear to come from a realistic source—a window, a lamp, a lantern, a flashlight, a miner's lamp, an overhead fixture—or from within the character's enlightened inner self. The source will narrow the cinematographer's options. After the long shot, the two-shot and single lighting has to match to be consistent with the lighting motivation. The strongest light becomes the *key*—a high diagonal light that defines the shape of the head and face. The *fill light*, which does not have to be motivated, softens the harsh shadow of the key and may throw light on the background. The *backlight* separates the actor from the background so the scene appears to have three dimensions. Making the backlight a little stronger than normal tends to glamorize the actor with a halo of light.

The lighting of the long shot is different from that of the close-up in that the lights are usually high and strong—too harsh for the close-up. But sometimes, when there are animals or children in the scene who cannot easily match their action in the long shot and close-up, it is necessary to shoot both types of shots at the same time, using two cameras. And when doing stunts or car crashes, it is often advisable to use two cameras or even more.

The most practical lights for filming on location are the Lowellights, which can be folded to fit into one or two suitcases. Ross Lowell, the inventor and manufacturer of this line, has been a location cameraman for many years. I made several films with him, including two that were nominated for an Oscar, and watched his line of products evolve over the years, culminating in an Oscar for Technical Achievement. In developing equipment, Lowell has emphasized portability and pragmatism. His light stands are made of aluminum instead of heavier steel. He replaced sandbags, which were employed to stabilize light stands, with plastic bottles that can be filled with water then emptied again for easier storage and portability. He replaced the huge steel softlight, which probably weighed fifty pounds, for a fixture of a few pounds. He designed a foldable aluminum piece to fit over a door on which you can place a light, eliminating the need for a stand. The equipment, sold and rented worldwide, is constantly evolving.

Outdoor lighting is not easy. Direct, overhead sunlight must be balanced with reflectors or filtered with a lighting tent. It is common to use electric lights outdoors for fill or backlight. Cinematographers prefer shooting wide shots in the morning or evening when the light is low and the shape of the scenery is more beautiful from cross-lighting.

Lighting is a very complicated subject, and we must be content with covering the rudiments here. (See appendix III for books on the subject.)

Assistant Director (AD)

The AD is like a cook. He or she coordinates all elements of production so they are ready for the shot at the same time. The AD is constantly checking the time, asking for forecasts of when each department will be ready, trying to keep to schedule so ideally, the lighting will be finished at the same time that the actors have finished with costume and makeup and had a run-through for lines. The AD also breaks down the script, schedules the work, and supervises all production assistants (PAs).

The AD is particularly involved in planning moves from one location to another. He or she is responsible for clearing the next location, making sure that the crew is expected, and giving their estimated time of arrival. The AD should know where parking is available and should collect the parking tickets for all vehicles parked illegally. Unpaid people should not have to pay fines.

The AD phones all the people the night before shooting with news about the advance schedule. He or she should pass out the daily shooting schedule each morning. If an actor has a schedule conflict—say, an important audition—the AD should try to resolve the problem to everyone's satisfaction.

Assistant Cinematographer (AC)

This crew member works only on film, not on videotape. The AC loads magazines, empties and cans film, labels the cans, keeps a log of the shooting, installs and removes lenses, measures focus, and follows focus when there is movement or a change of focal plane. Further duties include moving the camera and tripod from one setup to another, repositioning it, packing and unpacking the camera and camera gear. In short, the AC tries to anticipate the needs of the cinematographer.

Video Engineer

In the days when video cameras had tubes, the engineer dealt with the tubes and set the color for the camera. Now, in the era of chip cameras, the engineer's main responsibility is to record sound. In addition, he or she carries and sets up the camera, changing lenses and following focus. The engineer also sets the color controls and frees up the cinematographer to concentrate on lighting.

Script Clerk

Also known as the continuity director or dialogue director, the script clerk makes sure that the dialogue, performance, makeup, costumes, and props are consistent from one shot to the next. For example, a character wearing a hat while walking toward a building in one shot should not be hatless in the next shot, filmed several days later. Directional continuity is discussed in the next chapter because it is a directorial concern more than the script clerk's. It is storytelling more than consistency from scene to scene. The script clerk does prompt the director, but his or her specific responsibilities are the following:

Dialogue Continuity: The script clerk notes any variations in the dialogue and clears any change with the director. For instance, say that in take one the performance is good, but the actor has changed a line because of forgetfulness or improvisation. Other takes are done but with the text as written, and for some reason the director prefers the improvised version. The script clerk then tells the actor how the text was changed so that he or she will duplicate the words when coverage (closer shots) begins. Normally, the wide or long shot is done first and the closer shots come later. The script clerk also conducts dialogue rehearsals with the actors before a take.

Performance Continuity: For starters, the intensity of a performance should be consistent from take to take. The script clerk should take notes on the actors' movements—when

they turn, step, sit, and so forth. Gestures and behavior such as cigarette smoking also must be noted—when the actor strikes a match, takes a puff, flicks the ashes, where the actor holds the cigarette and with which hand. Smoking and other actions will vary from take to take, especially when you are dealing with an inexperienced actor. Therefore, you (the director), the actor, and the script clerk need to come to a decision on which line of the script the character is to smoke or cook or set the table.

Ideally, the actor asks the director which take they are matching to. If it's "take three," the script clerk should have notes on where the cigarette was on which line, when the turn was made, when the glasses came off, and so forth. Some actors have training that includes improvisation and get so carried away when they act that they cannot duplicate their performance to ensure matching coverage. For this kind of actor—and for children who may be too young to understand the concept of matching action—you may need to shoot cutaways to get from take to take. A *cutaway* looks like a logical shot in the sequence but is actually in the sequence only to cut away from the actor speaking when the actor flubs. Maybe the cutaway is a "hand prop" such as a briefcase or a bunch of flowers, a clock or a dog cocking its head. If it is a two-person scene and you are doing close-ups, you can try cutting to the other person listening or talking in order to avoid a mismatch.

Makeup Continuity: If an actor has a cut lip and you break for lunch before doing the close-up, the script clerk needs to make sure his lip is still noticeably cut after lunch so he looks the same in both shots. In this case, the best approach would be to take a polaroid when the director says "cut" and refer to it when getting ready for the close-up after lunch. Any other special makeup, such as a black eye, a scar, or a suntan, will also have to be duplicated after a break. Such circumstances are more likely to be

found in a professional union situation, where interruptions are more common—if the crew doesn't break for lunch, for example, there's a meal penalty.

Costume Continuity: The script clerk notes what costume the actor is wearing, checks whether it is for the right day, and notes any changes that have occurred in the look of the costume. If two children are filmed playing in the mud on Monday and their entrance into the house after playing is shot on Thursday, the mud must be the same in both shots.

Prop and Set Continuity: Problems in this area commonly occur when there is a lot of physical action in a scene and props get thrown or moved around. Problems may also arise in the event of reshoots some days or weeks later. In both cases, taking a polaroid of original prop positions is the best guarantee of a rapid reassembly to conform to the original setup. Before shooting a close-up of a prop that is moved—let's say a ring that is placed on a finger—the director and the script clerk must note how the prop is handled in the long shot. Note that the ring is held in the right hand, that the left hand holds the ring hand of the person getting the ring, that the hand is turned toward the camera, and so forth.

Gaffer

Also called the electrician, this is the person who places the lights, focusing them where the cinematographer indicates, working closely with him or her to establish the mood, and then breaks down the equipment. After shooting is over, he or she repacks the lights and cable so they are ready for the next setup, the next move, or for a return to the rental house or school equipment department. The gaffer finds power and makes sure that the fuses

do not blow. He or she splits 220-amp lines into 110 for normal lights. When a generator is needed, the gaffer runs it.

Gaffers are frequently creative and artistic, anticipating the objectives of the cinematographer. Sometimes the gaffer and cinematographer speak to each other in the language of light, and the gaffer will perhaps add or subtract a scrim on a light simply by reading the expression of the cinematographer. When shooting outdoors, the gaffer holds and focuses the reflectors. In a small crew, the gaffer is often helped by the grip. In an even smaller crew, the gaffer *is* the grip. In making *Jonathan's Turn*, the gaffer was also the sound man.

Grip

A grip does any rigging that needs to be done—attaching a camera to a car, securing the camera to scaffolding, pushing a dolly, building any devices for the set, securing an actor on a ledge. The grip also secures lights that have to be specially mounted or stabilized, holds reflectors, moves vehicles, and helps the gaffer.

Sound Mixer

The sound mixer records the sound, after choosing the microphones—lavolier, radio, boom, shotgun—and controls a mixer if there is more than one microphone. He or she often works with a boom operator but just as often works alone, controlling the gain or volume, as well as operating the boom. The sound mixer approves the location for sound and installs baffles, or sound blankets, to absorb street noise or echoes in the room.

Unlike the other members of the crew whose work is more

visible, the mixer is often taken for granted unless he or she specifically tells the director there is a problem. This is a mistake. You must check to hear for yourself what sound you are getting and whether there is a problem. You may have an AC hum from crossed wires or "boominess," a slight echo from a boom being placed too far from the speaker. If you do not know your sound person to be a reliable and self-critical craftsperson, listen to the scenes with earphones until your trust is won.

Costume Designer

Obviously, this is the person who selects or designs and makes costumes. He or she also does any special sewing—for example, for breakaway (loosely stitched) costumes, which are to be ripped off. Costumes are hung in a reserved closet, and actors should never be permitted to wear theirs home even if the clothing belongs to them. Every costume is labeled with the name of the character and a number denoting the day of the story on which the costume is worn. The costumer also notes any changes in the look of a costume from scene to scene and works with the script clerk to prevent mismatches, since the latter has more experience in this area.

Prop Person

In a major production, the prop person serves under the art director, but most beginning filmmakers do without the latter. Therefore, questions of taste, color selection, and coordination fall to the person doing props, in association with the director and/or cinematographer. The prop person not only rounds up the props but also returns them to their owners.

Whoever is doing props should make a master prop list. You, as the director, should underline in your shooting script the props already mentioned and in the margin note other props necessary for the scene. Your prop person will be too busy to attend rehearsals, but either you or your assistant should make note of any props that you have added. The prop person should have the confidence to go beyond the list and suggest other props. There should be a props room or closet with one box for the props of each set. As the prop person gathers items, a tiny label should be placed on the bottom of each prop or somewhere out of sight of the camera with a number and the lender's name and address, if possible. If you have a lot of props, you will need a log such as the following:

PROP	Rent.	Purch.	Loan	Lender
picture #1			X	Lord Antique Store . . .
Patik watch		X		Gingold Jewelry . . .
golf sticks			X	Herman Burton . . .
sofa	$10 per day			Wilson Furniture . . .

Makeup

The makeup person should be sure that none of the actors is made up much darker or lighter than other members of the cast in the same shots. African Americans require a somewhat darker powder and should be photographed against darker backgrounds, if possible, to reduce contrast. For me, the point to remember is that makeup should not be done at the last minute so that I don't find myself with everything ready except the makeup—wasting valuable time.

A film set may give the appearance of chaos as all these members of the crew do their work. The person who gives their work meaning is the director, who through the crew, the equipment, the actors, and, later, the editor, tells a story in order to reach an audience and give them an experience. Let's now look at how the director uses the camera to enhance the story.

13

▰▰▰▰▰▰▰▰▰▰▰▰▰

Directing
the
Camera

THE DIRECTOR TALKS TO THE AUDIENCE in the language of cinema: "Watch this long shot of cars booming along the parkway below. We're panning up now. The camera is framing a town. Looks like a bedroom community. The camera is panning past houses to the filling station. The camera is now zooming to the filling station to let you know that this story starts here. A car pulls up.

"The transaction with the attendant does not seem normal. The shots of the customer are very close. The music is ominous. The attendant and the customer look at each other with distrust. The customer drives away and the attendant goes back to the garage, but the camera keeps on zooming into the pump while that dramatic music grows louder. Maybe the pump will explode. It does! Now the story's off and running. Why did it happen? Who are these people? Cut to the customer driving away, looking vengeful. Will he get away with it? Back to the filling station. What happened to the attendant? Lying on the pavement, surrounded by flames, liquid spreading toward him. . . ." The visual storytelling has drawn the viewer into a story.

Camera Moves

After visual storytelling, working with the camera and the cast comes next on a director's list of requisites. What does the camera see? When does it move and why? This is what you have to be clear about. Here are the moves a camera can make.

Pan: Short for *panorama*, this term indicates a lateral move of the camera, rotating on a tripod, a dolly, or a shoulder. Many people use the term *pan up* or *pan down* when they mean *tilt up* and *tilt down.*

Dolly: The dolly is a hand-pushed vehicle on which the camera is mounted, with a seat for the operator. It is frequently fitted with a boom arm which can be used to reposition the shot. A hydraulic mechanism allows the camera operator to boom up or down during a shot for a dramatic change of camera perspective. Often the camera can move forward or backward and up or down at the same time if you have an exceptional operator and dolly pusher. The boom capability enables the camera to smoothly recompose the shot during a movement so that the camera is dollying and booming at the same time an actor is sitting down or getting up. The moviola dolly, the industry standard, can also crabbe, that is, move on a diagonal, and is often called the Crabbe dolly.

In student productions and other low-budget films, the dolly may be improvised. It could be a wheelchair or a hospital gurney. Or the cinematographer can handhold the camera, usually fitted with a wide-angle lens, walking either behind or ahead of the actor. With practice, the camera operator learns to move fluidly.

The late Michael Livesey, with whom I worked for twenty years, moved up and down as if he had hydraulic fluid in his veins.

Zoom Lens: Everyone knows the terms *zoom in* and *zoom out.* The zoom lens is a variable focal-length lens that operates either with a small motor or manually by rotating a zoom handle. The lens either widens (i.e., shows a fuller visual field) or tightens (i.e., moves toward an object, narrowing the visual field). Many viewers find fast zooms jarring. Additionally, fast zooms give the illusion that the field is rushing to the camera. By contrast, with the less-mechanical dolly effect, the inquisitive camera moves gracefully into a detail or a close-up. Zooms of any speed do not resemble dolly moves because there are no passing objects or people during the move.

Wide-angle Lenses: The normal lens in 16mm filming is the 25mm. With it, the camera will see a scene approximating what the human eye sees. Wider angles are 16mm lenses, 12mm lenses, and so on, down to the fisheye lens that sees a very wide but distorted field. All wide-angle lenses distort the field, making objects close to the camera seem very large and exaggerating the distance of those farther away. Such lenses can be used for comic or grotesque effect, or can be used to create the illusion of covering a very wide area. A wide-angle lens is preferable to a normal lens when you want to get a full shot of a building without having to back up so far you'd be shooting in the middle of traffic.

Long Lens: This lens gives a telescopic effect called fore-shortening. It creates the opposite effect of a wide-angle lens, where the scene seems to be spread out. The long lens seems to compress the distance between foreground and background and makes people running toward the camera seem as if they are not getting anywhere. This effect often fits the story line. Or the director who wants to "steal" a scene (shoot cars and pedestrians without obtaining signed release forms) might use a long lens to shoot two actors, wired with radio mikes, crossing the street. Styles in directing change, and it seems to me that I saw this sort of cinematography in the sixties more than I do today. Often when the technology is first available, it is overused and then dropped in favor of something new. Several years ago, telephoto lenses were popular on *Hill Street Blues*, giving the viewer the impression of seeing a busy, crowded, chaotic police station. Currently, long lenses are used on *NYPD Blue*.

Types of Camera Shots

Moving Master Shot: This sort of seamless shot, from the POV of either a furtive character or an omniscient camera, moves through grass and trees, often glides through walls, changing focus and frame size constantly. Experimentally, Hitchcock used nine such takes to make *Rope*. (Each take lasted ten minutes, the equivalent of one reel in 35mm.) I saw a Claude Chabrol film where the camera was in constant motion for several minutes. In a professional film, the camera is usually on a dolly, and the skill of the dolly grip is very important in carrying out the director's moves. The camera could also be on a small studio crane or a Steadicam, a device that stabilizes the handheld camera as the operator walks. In a very good student film by Peter Judson, I recently saw very effective use of a Steadicam by Steve Consentino. These moving camera shots can also be done in a wheelchair with the cinematographer handholding and wearing a shoulder brace. Sometimes these shots can be effective in slowly revealing frightening information to the audience in mounting fashion.

Stationary Master: This is known as the long shot where the cinematographer can tilt, pan, or change frame size with the zoom, but often the frame does not change much. The shot is used to orient the viewer geographically or to show action that would easily go out of frame in closer shots. Often the director and editor use a reference shot such as this to get from one take to another.

Group Shot or Full Shot: Closer on the actors than the geographic long shot, the group or full shot does not usually frame much architecture. Its purpose is to capture dialogue in scenes where the interaction among people is important.

Two-Shot: As you would expect, the two-shot shows relationships between people. There are two types of these shots: the fifty-fifty and the over-the-shoulder shot. In the fifty-fifty, which is used a lot in TV sitcoms, both actors are facing each other. Such a shot does not allow the actors to make eye contact with the audience and is therefore dramatically weaker than the second kind of two-shot. In the over-the-shoulder shot, two complementary shots are made, each favoring one of the two actors. In a variation on the over-the-shoulder shot, the character in the foreground does not look directly at the other character but is guided by the director to motivate a look in a direction that will show his or her profile. In life, as in film, people in conversation do not stare at each other continuously while talking. They look away and then back. Such a shot is useful if the characters are talking at the same time, stepping on each other's lines. Overlaps are normal and lifelike, but when you shoot matching over-the-shoulder shots planning to cut to the speaker, the overlaps present a problem because usually one character will be on mike and the other will be off mike. Thus, most actors are directed to avoid overlaps. If they are necessary for the scene, the overlap can be edited on the sound track later.

Close-up: Sometimes called a single, this shot is used for increased dramatic intensity, character development, and important dialogue. An extreme close-up is reserved for special moments of greater intensity and change. Sometimes these shots are used for caressing a beautiful face or increasing sympathy for a character or trying to go inside his or her soul.

Panning Shot: Directors like to get actors on their feet for indoor scenes, and the camera often follows a moving actor by panning. I am talking about a shot that is smaller than a geographic master. Let's say a host seats a guest on a couch, then goes to the bar to get her a drink. The problem is to keep both actors in the same shot. This can be done by zooming to a three-quarter view of the host and zooming back as he reenters the shot. If the guest has important dialogue, you can then make a separate setup for her. Close-ups are difficult when the character is moving because the actors move out of focus or out of the frame.

Follow Shot: Also called a *tracking shot*, from the days when dolly tracks were laid. If you shot the above scene by following the host with a dolly move (or a zoom), you would dolly back toward the bar and then perhaps stop and pan with him as he went to the bar. This kind of shot is very useful for seeing the expression on the actor's face if his face is at odds with his words. Whether you use a pan or a follow shot should depend on which dialogue you regard as important and which character you want the audience to watch. Follow shots are also used for characters riding in cars and other vehicles: The camera is set up on the hood of the car to shoot through the windshield, or can be rigged on the front passenger door.

Shooting for the Cutting Room

When you get to the cutting room, the reasons for redundant coverage—shooting the scene from different angles—will become obvious. Since most short films end up on TV (if the filmmaker is lucky), close-ups are essential in every scene—TV is a close-up medium. Dialogue is easier to shorten later if covered in close-ups. As you get firmer in your craft, you will not cover everything but will make decisions about what to cover in advance of shooting. Suppose you have a scene of several minutes in which a teacher moves to the front of a class and calms down the students, and ends when the bell rings. You need a long shot only at the beginning and the end of the scene. In between you need group shots, two-shots, and singles as the students interact with the teacher. Let the dialogue guide you. If one student has a long speech that has to be intercut with an intense shot of the teacher, cover that student with group shots and singles. This sort of surefooted "editing in the camera" saves time in shooting, syncing, and editing.

On the other hand, if you have some nagging doubts about a scene that may be overlong or have doubts about a performance in that scene, you may have to cover it thoroughly so that the decisions can be made in the editing room.

Axis

The axis, an imaginary line running through the frame from top to bottom, is a crucial concept in filmmaking. In a single shot of one person, the axis line runs through the face, allotting a little more "negative" or extra space on one side of the face. If the actor is looking left to right (L–R for short), there should be a little more space on the right than the left. You must make sure that all shots of the actor taken against the same background and in the same context are in agreement. Even if the actor rotates his or her head, it should not be rotated past the axis unless you purposely change the axis by staging a cross to new positions, and then everything must be kept consistent with the new axis.

In a two-shot, the axis line divides the screen roughly in half. This means that all other shots of the same actor(s) must agree with the previous shot. The most common way of shooting two people talking to each other when they are not moving is to shoot over-the-shoulder shots, mentioned earlier. These keep one character on the left and the other on the right. When you finish shooting with the angle favoring character 1, who is looking left to right, have your cinematographer come around to shoot a complementary angle over character 2's shoulder. When coming around, the cinematographer must keep the characters on the same side of the axis line: character 1 still looks left to right and character 2 looks right to left. Keep the size of the characters the same in each shot as well.

If the characters are standing and facing each other, you can use the fifty-fifty shot, or, if the twosome is moving toward the camera, both looking ahead and at each other, you shoot them head-on. Then if you want to switch to single shots, of course, you keep the orientation the same, with the character on the left looking L–R and the character on the right looking R–L.

For further explanation of the axis, see *Grammar of the Film Language*, listed in appendix III.

Directional Continuity: The movement of people when walking, driving, flying, and the like, is also kept consistent R–L and L–R. Similarly, if you are filming the story of a young man from a small town who is determined to leave for the city no matter what, show him moving in one direction when he shows determination and makes progress and in the opposite direction when he is beset by obstacles that propel him back to his hometown. This type of directional continuity is aimed at the audience's subconscious.

Sergei Eisenstein established the convention of showing one army in *Aleksandr Nevsky* moving from right to left and the opposing army moving from left to right. In a boxing match, of course, the boxers will rotate as they fight, but when the bell clangs one boxer should go to his corner and glower R–L while the other looks vengefully L–R. By the same token, if two people are talking on the telephone, one should look L–R and the other R–L. When this material is edited, the boxers will be glowering at each other rather than the audience. The people on the telephone will be looking at each other as if they were in the same room, rather than facing away from each other.

Deciding What to Match: You could drive yourself crazy trying to match every action in every retake. Instead, decide in advance how you are going to cut the scene. Tell the script clerk where the cut is so the actor knows what movement has to match. Don't give the actor more than a couple of continuity instructions because it's too much to remember in addition to everything else on the actor's mind. Once you get to close-ups, matching action is usually less important than matching readings, expressions, or text.

Suppose you are directing a scene where two people enter a living room, talking and carrying their drinks, then sit in chairs and continue talking. You might want to carry the master shot until they sit down. The first chance you have to cover the dialogue is after they sit. In take one of the master, the character who is speaking grabs the arms of a chair, leans forward, and sits.

In the tighter shot, the actor does not grab the arms of the chair and lean forward. You do not have to reshoot to get a match. You can cut to the sitting shot after the actor is settled, or you can cut to the chair before he sits—and you will not have a mismatch. You use one or the other, but do not have to use both. This is known in the film trade as the "either/or."

Here is another example with a time-saving observation. The above action continues, and the second character throws his drink into the face of the first character. You can save time if you film the scene as follows: start coverage shooting over the shoulder of the first man, who gets the drink thrown at him; cover the throwing in the shot favoring the second man and cut before the throwing gesture is completed; begin the close-up of the first man when the drink lands on the face. The other option would be to film all the action using a wider shot. But then it would take ten or fifteen minutes to prepare for a retake: you would have to towel-dry and then blow-dry the actor's hair, provide a new shirt or iron it, perhaps supply a new tie. In this instance of "either/or," it is obviously much easier for you to match to the close-up in the first setup.

Coverage

Once you have staged your action, in rehearsal, it is time to make notes in your script on how you will cover the action—which scenes you will duplicate and overlap (by shooting from different angles and with a variety of camera shots) and which you will not. Bring these notes to a rehearsal for the benefit of the cinematographer, so you can get his or her input on the shooting plan. It's a good idea to have the cinematographer do some shooting of this rehearsal on 8mm without any lighting. You can later discuss the best way to cover the scene while looking at a monitor.

In addition to planning camera shots, cuts, and matches, the director makes other preparations for shooting, such as picking locations and making schedules. These will be considered in the next chapter.

14

■■■■■■■■■■■■■■■

Preparing
for the
Shoot

Saving Time

Preparation is the key to speed during production. The time you
save by shooting efficiently will convert to more setups for cutting
room choices and less actor fatigue. You cannot take a lot of time
with every setup. You have to know which scenes will pay off and
those decisions should be made in advance.

An inherent danger in making movies is the temptation to
spend a long time on the master (very little of which is usable),
then to shoot the group shots, the over-the-shoulders, and the
close-ups at the end of the day. This is when your stars' concentration begins to flag and they look their worst. Particularly if you
plan to reach the audience with the tight shots, shoot them as
early in the day as possible.

Picking Locations

The most important thing about a location is its resonance—its
capacity to add visual meaning to your film. The homespun,

working-class sets of *Time Expired* reinforce the conventions and norms that Bobby departed from in bonding with his transvestite prison cellmate. The hills, plazas, and fountains of *Skater Dater*, the cockney neighborhood of *End of the Rainbow*, the bucolic setting of Ron Ellis's humane *Board and Care*, the gloomy pastoral and Bergmanesque settings of *The Dove*, the suburban, well-kept yuppie home in *Kaboom*—each contributes to the illusion that the characters actually belong in these sets.

An indoor location should be somewhat larger than a normal-sized room because the lens narrows it down. The ceiling should be high enough to allow for operating a sound boom and for hanging lights or putting them on stands. A great deal of the room is taken up with the tripod or dolly, the crew, and other legitimate onlookers. The location should be quiet; away from traffic or neighborhood noise, or the sound of frequent airplanes. Your sound person should check out the location for echoes, and there should be space to hang sound blankets around the acting area.

When you have chosen your principal location, be sure that you can also shoot some of your minor scenes there as well as your crucial scenes. You will need green rooms in which actors can make up, change costumes, and rest. You should also be able to designate one room as the production office, where you can install additional telephones for the period of the shoot. This room should be far enough from the sets so that talking on the phone does not get recorded. Or rent a portable phone, possibly from the same place where you rent walkie-talkies (which you will need for communication between crew and AD, especially outdoors).

Be a penny pincher! Don't buy or rent what you can get free with a mention in the credits. Big companies often have someone in the PR department who deals with exchanges of free services for credit or prominent display of the company name.

Production Script

Take a fresh copy of your reading script and start marking it up. Give every scene a number and a name, using minimal words (e.g., "Grandpa gets drunk" or "Mom gets fired"). The numbers and the names will later appear on your shooting schedule. Underline all locations and make a separate list of them so you will be able to add up shooting time at each one. (Selecting locations and moving from one location to another are discussed later in the chapter.) Ask your cinematographer for his or her input. Make another list of actors, the ones you cast in your film and the runners-up—just in case. Make notes about any unusual production problems, such as special makeup, breakaway props, car wrecks, and so forth. Underline props specified in the script, and note those that are indispensable so you can shoot them first. Next go through your script and at the end of every scene write in the number of hours you estimate it will take to shoot. Show this to your cinematographer to get his or her agreement. Go through the script once more and note when a new day starts as far as costumes are concerned. Make notes on the costumes needed in each scene (number them).

Coordinating Costumes

Pass along your notes on the costumes to the costumer and have him or her come in for a meeting with you and the cinematographer. If the actors will be supplying their own costumes, have them bring their selections to this meeting. Make sure that actors who will perform together are costume-checked together. You wouldn't want everyone in the scene to wear red, for example. In your costume room or area, your costumer can put all the day 1 costumes on the same rack with labels in large print which can be removed before shooting.

Establishing the Shooting Schedule

For each scene, you have already noted on your production script the scene number and name (e.g., "Grandpa gets drunk"), any special props or stunts, the number of hours you think it will take to shoot, and the costume day on which the scene takes place. Transfer this information to a separate table of contents, which serves as your point of reference when you prepare your shooting schedule. The AD paces the production according to the speed of the crew and cast, but in general, you should aim for shooting three pages a day.

Each day's shooting schedule should look something like this:

DAILY SCHEDULE

March 18

D'S BEDROOM

SCENE	HRS	SC DESCRIPTION	COSTUMES
SC. 3 D	3 HOURS	Deborah calls Grandma	Day 1
SC. 21 D	2 HOURS	Scratcher wakes Deborah	Day 5

lunch 1:30

SC. 5 N   3 HOURS   Scratcher and Evelyn   Day 2
                                                    fight

Sound: Boom mike

Props: sc. 5 pillow fight

(get 6 feather pillows plus vacuum cleaner after each take)

Stunts: sc. 5 floor padding, knee and elbow padding

Transp: p.u. Jenifer Logan train station 8:39 A.M.

MOVE TO HOSPITAL Set up sc. 20 for A.M.

ADVANCE SCHEDULE:

March 19

SC. 20, 28, 31 HOSP.

MOVE TO PARK

SC. 35 sunset walk around lake

The point of all this paperwork is to ensure that everyone is singing from the same hymnbook. You will find as a director that people are always coming up to you and asking what the next scene is—even when it is already in writing. Often people lose or misplace their schedules and/or scripts. But in production, mistakes are costly in time and money. Just think of the mischief that can be caused by one incorrectly labeled costume.

After thoroughly reviewing the production script, you'll be able to budget your film and see where your money and time are going. Are they going toward the things most likely to win an audience? Or do you have some scenes or passages that are too expensive for your budget? If so, simplify your script. It is easier to do it now than to go to the time and expense of shooting scenes and then see them end up on the cutting room floor.

Supplying Food and Beverages

Even if you are not paying your crew with money, you can pay them with compliments and with food and treats. Keep the coffeepot going, and supply donuts and bagels in the morning. Keep energy drinks on hand, which people will appreciate in the afternoon. If everyone goes to different restaurants on lunch break, you can be delayed getting restarted in the afternoon. As a time-saving alternative, see if you can get a cherished friend to arrange lunches, either by bringing in menus and taking orders early in the morning or by purchasing food for a self-service buffet. Find out your crew's preferences (Thai food and sushi are current favorites) by passing out cards for each person to fill out. Don't go in for heavy meals, which take time to digest and drain energy from the production. Set up a salad bar, including a few frills like avocado, sardines, sushi, and pasta. Another day you could have sandwich makings with fruit juice.

Just before the lunch break, you should let your crew know what the first shot after lunch will be. The same is true for when you break at the end of the day: Give them the first shot for the next morning. This avoids the problem of people sitting around idly until they are told what to do.

Moving From Location to Location

Plan your changes of location carefully. A move is a great time eater and should be done only after a day of shooting or, in the worst-case scenario, during the lunch hour. Ideally, the AD coordinates the move, spelling out all details—who is driving which vehicle, who are the passengers, and so forth. If the move will take place during the lunch hour, the AD should give an early lunch break to those people who can be spared from the shooting of the last shots. They can then eat and get ready for the move. (This is an especially important day to have lunch on the set.)

If you are going to shoot an outdoor scene, put parking instructions on the schedule so that everyone does not park in your shot. This way you avoid spending the first hour of the morning reparking cars. Equip drivers with maps and all useful phone numbers. If the vehicles are traveling together, travel in caravan style with lights on even during the day, and keep your eyes trained on the car following yours in the rearview mirror.

Getting Signed Releases

Your cast and extras should sign release forms granting permission to be filmed. You can put a PA (production assistant) in charge of collecting them before the cameras start rolling. I find that if a lawyer draws up a release form, it gives all your extras a headache trying to read it. Follow the KISS principle (Keep It Simple, Students) by creating a straightforward document such as the following:

LEGAL RELEASE FORM

For good and valuable consideration, hereby acknowledged, I consent to the use of my face and voice in the film

_____ ,

no matter which medium is used to transmit it—nontheatrical, TV, cable, or subsequently developed technology.

(signed) _____

(guardian) _____

Address _____

Witness _____

Witness _____

Date _____

Directing is full of the unpredictable. The cast gets sick or changes plans, locations fall away, new costs arise, the lab goofs, wonderful people do not get along, and so forth, leaving you to improvise contingency plans. On the other hand, there are often pleasant surprises. The actors work out much better than expected. The weather is accommodating. The cinematographer outdoes himself or herself to please you.

When things start to go wrong, when your feelings are hurt and it is hard to bounce back, think of what is best for your audience. Any discomfort you may feel during shooting will be overpowered later when your audience has a good time watching your film.

I have devoted a great deal of space to *Jonathan's Turn* in its various stages of development. At first, I wrote the script only for this book, but my assistant, Leslie Holland, strongly suggested that I make the film. There are many lessons that I encountered during production, which I pass on to you in the next chapter.

15

▮▮▮▮▮▮▮▮▮▮▮▮▮▮▮

Producing *Jonathan's Turn*

Casting the Actors

Many say that casting is 50 percent of directing. Many say the percentage is higher. Certainly, in making this short, I found the actors to be of crucial importance. In fact, because the leads were so young, I made a deal with myself: If I could not find two great actors, I would not do the film. I then placed the following ad in *Backstage*, the casting newspaper:

Short film needs
6-year-old boy who goes from sad to glad—lead. Can be older. Harpo-like 5-year-old boy must be able to cry and scream on cue. Winning grin.

No pay, great experience. Oscar-winning director. Send photo.

Films By Edmond Levy, Inc.
135 Central Park West
New York City 10023

Responding to this ad were a lot of undisciplined children, most of whom could not read or remember the text or had coloring wildly different from that of Chris Norris, the actor I had in mind to play the father. I decided to widen my search by violating one of my own rules: Don't use SAG actors. I checked with SAG and learned that I could offer the actors an experimental film contract, which meant that I paid them nothing immediately and the rest when and if the film earned money. I thought the terms were fair, and I called a company called Breakdown Service, which notifies all the agents of roles that are open.

As a result, I met seven-year-old Trent Sage, who could memorize lines quickly, keep his concentration, and discuss the character. Now I had a Jonathan, but I didn't see anyone right for the part of Danny. None of the boys could scream and cry on cue. It was a tall order and I was about ready to cancel the film . . . when Jacob Penn came to audition. At age five, he had great understanding, enthusiasm, and the ability to scream his head off on cue. Clearly he was not a parent-dominated actor, and his love for the script and for acting was very clear. So the film was on.

Meanwhile, during the auditions I had been listening to my dialogue. I found it thin, in need of beefing up. Otherwise the arguments would be over too soon and the characters would have no dimensions. I also told the mothers of the actors what the problem was: that the children stopped acting when they were not saying lines. They needed to behave like the characters, not just say their words. I told their mothers about this problem, and they were eager to help. Kyle Waters, the actress-mother of Jacob, was able to assist him in preparing for his role, and Trent's mother, Beverly Sage, who did not have a theatrical background, hired an acting coach for her son.

In the end, the boys gave polished performances. Trent was successful in the role of Jonathan not just because he read his lines well but because his expressions communicated his feelings—he looks proud when he gives his father's time schedule correctly, for instance. Danny's yelp of triumph when the mother favors him over his brother was not in the script. It probably came right from Jacob's heart.

Kyle read the lines of the mother in rehearsal, but she sounded too reasonable and sane. When I found an actress with a very neurotic quality, Kyle accepted the decision graciously.

Filming the Action

I was fortunate in that a former student of mine, Steve Wolf, now a very able and well-known stuntman, offered to be the stunt coordinator just for expenses. Since he lives in Memphis, we worked by phone and fax until a week before the shooting when he came to New York to prep.

During the near-accidents, the limo was actually being pulled by a tow truck. What Trent did with the steering wheel had no effect on the wheels. Steve sat in the chauffeur's seat, wearing the chauffeur's uniform so that our shots of his hands and body would match those of the actor playing the role of the chauffeur. I sat in the backseat watching the action through the rearview mirror. Ross Lowell, my consultant/director of photography, filmed these as profile shots while sitting on a sling suspended from the limo with the door open. This position was painful to Ross, and we tried to work quickly. When we shot through the front window of the car, Ross was tied to the hood with fabric fastened to suction cups.

When we were shooting the car-in-traffic sequence, I was sitting next to Trent, screaming "YOU'RE GOING TO HIT YOUR MOTHER!" When he veered in the other direction, I screamed "THAT'S YOUR SISTER, IDIOT!" One way or another, we got him to turn off his titillated smile and look alarmed.

The stunts were choreographed and rehearsed with professional stunt drivers. Even the woman driving a car out of a driveway was a stunt driver friend of Steve's. As he was laying out the collision of the limo and the UPS hand truck, which he had built out of pipes, Steve drew a chalk mark in the middle of the street so that the limo (which he would be driving, wearing the chauffeur's hat) would never cross over to the side where the UPS truck went. Max Maxwell, who played the UPS man, was protected in his backward fall by wearing stuntman gear that resembles football gear.

Location "Cheats"

The original plans were to shoot the Washington, D.C., scenes in Washington. This would have added transportation and per diem costs to the budget. Then Steve Wolf gave me the idea of shooting the stunt work in the New York area and the D.C. driving shots in Central Park. When two juxtaposed shots look like the same location but are actually shot on different days in different locations, it is called a *cheat*, something that has to be carefully planned. We rented the limo in New York, used it in Long Island for the stunt shots, then kept it to drive a skeleton crew down to Washington, saving $1,200 in airfares.

The stunts that were supposed to take place in residential Washington were actually shot in the hometown of associate

producer Leslie Holland, whose parents' house was comman-
deered for a green room, office, changing room, and refectory. In
Washington, we worked with a police liaison, who sent us a D.C.
decal to place over the Nassau Police car and a patch to put on the
blue shirt worn by the actor playing the D.C. cop. Since we had
only one of each, we had to plan shots of the shirt and the car so
that the cheat would work. In Washington, at the Capitol, we
made a long shot of the steps and matched them to a courthouse in
New York. We shot the limo dropping the father off at the White
House with me in a dark suit standing in for actor Chris Norris.
We shot the approach to the D.C. airport in the limo driven by the
senator in Central Park, shooting through the windshield, and
then cut to a shot made in D.C. where the limo drives into a long
shot of the D.C. airport. We followed this by a takeoff shot made
at Kennedy Airport some weeks later. The cheats saved money but
consumed a lot of time.

In the original script, father and son get on an airplane that
develops tire and engine problems. As you can see in the treatment, the stewardess announces that the takeoff will be in just a
few minutes while the camera zooms past Mike and Jonathan to
the outside, where frantic technicians with toolboxes are climbing
the ladder to the plane. Naively, I began preparation with the
belief that we could get an airline to cooperate in shooting these
scenes and that if we could not, there would be plenty of stock
footage to solve our problem.

Was I wrong! I cannot count the number of urgent faxes,
pleading letters, and plot summaries sent to England (to British
Airways, where we thought we had an in) and to Washington for
permission to shoot in a plane. We tried two airlines, then drove
to a studio in Long Island that had a mock-up (they wanted
hundreds of dollars per row of seats). In the end, all we had was

an offer to shoot in the New York terminal lobby for $500 per hour.

Finally, a week before shooting, I changed the script so that father and son went to Washington without the film ever showing them getting on or off a plane. I figured that we could get stock footage of takeoffs and landings from the airlines or at least from a stock footage house. But the airlines did not have stock shots, and the stock footage houses charged too much money just to start looking. Clinging to the desire to have a takeoff shot, I went to La Guardia and Kennedy Airports three times. The winds change frequently, and good camera positions on the scouting day turned bad on the shooting day. Finally, postproduction cinematographer Brendon Creadle and I made an illicit shot from the roof of a JFK parking garage with just a few minutes of light left in the sky.

The principal eye on the set was Ross Lowell's. With Ross on board, we did not need an art director because he gave excellent suggestions for rearranging the furniture in my living room and dining room to improve it photographically.

It was Ross's idea to make a traveling shot of Jonathan riding in the toy car their father had given them, feeling a freedom he had never felt before. This shot set up his conflict with his brother over not getting a turn, and it set up the scene where he becomes a hero by driving. For this shot Ross made a special rigging so that the wheel of the car gave Trent (Jonathan) some resistance. Both Ross and Trent were mounted on a long red wagon rented from a plant nursery. Here again, we used a cheat. The traveling shot was done in Central Park; the close-up, a couple of weeks later at a second location; and five weeks after the first shot (from a moving station wagon in a third location) we did a shot of what Jonathan saw when he looked up—the sun glinting through tree branches.

Working with the Children

The children worked hard on the film. In California, you cannot work with a child more than two hours a day, although it is legally permissible in New York. But we paid a price for overworking them. Children cannot keep their concentration very long. They need rest and diversion. We would assign each child his own room with a TV and video games. Sometimes I felt that these games were what they *really* cared about. But the desire to shoot as much as possible drove me to extend the hours we worked. The children often got cranky or sullen. Either way, it was hard or impossible to work with them, and we had to switch to another scene or break for the day.

The boys fought constantly no matter how much they rested. We tried separating them until shooting, but only pleading and bribery worked in getting the two of them on the same set. Trent once walked off the picture, just as in Hollywood, but AD Terrence Duffy lured him back with the promise of a new video game. The tension worked for the scenes, but I would have preferred that it had been achieved by acting.

We also had to work around the children's auditions for national TV commercials. I was acutely aware that since I was not paying them a salary, I had best release them to audition for these lucrative commercials. Time and again, we would get a call from Trent's mother on her portable phone saying that she was just leaving the audition in a taxi and we could start lighting her son's shot.

Solutions to Unexpected Problems

Ross says I am the most pragmatic director he has ever worked with. I think maybe this comes from being a writer to whom revisions are the norm. Some of the time-consuming problems that I solved pragmatically might be useful to share here.

On the day we were supposed to shoot a scene in which Danny looks at his watch and the close-up shows that the crystal is smashed, we could not find the watch. Rather than lose time searching for it, I told Danny to show his bare wrist and say, "I didn't lose it. It's just gone."

Once we arrived at the Senate location (Federal Court Building in New York) with no one cast as the senator's secretary. I knew I had very little time to cast someone and get her ready for the scene. But I found a friend of Steve Wolf's waiting for him and immediately pressed her into service.

On another occasion, Chris Norris (the father) had to leave in the middle of the day to make a 1:00 P.M. court date in Brooklyn. Since we needed several shots of father and son in a cab, we ended up going with him to court, shooting half our cab scenes as we went. While he was in court, we broke for lunch, picked him up something to eat, and shot the other half of his taxi scenes on the way back to Manhattan.

Editing and Scoring the Film

When it came to approaching an editor, I remembered Gretta Miller, with whom I had recently worked on a TV promotion piece. On breaks she had spoken of her children, ages five and nine, with great affection, and I felt she was a natural for the film. She said she would edit the film for my low, low price if she could edit at home. Gretta started work after she had taken the children to school and volunteered there for an hour. When I arrived, she poured Chinese herbal tea for me, set out snacks, and then we started to work. She managed without an assistant, except for the three cats, one rabbit, and numerous gerbils who were constantly crossing the Steenbeck editing machine with the film in motion. She arranged playdates, booked her husband into construction crews, and attended to her children's after-school demands without losing her concentration on the film. Toward the end of the day, she would prepare her family's dinner in the kitchen adjoining the editing room, never missing a beat of her reediting talks with me.

Music is an integral part of every film. When Ross Lowell came up with his traveling closeup of Jonathan, I knew we needed something to justify extending these shots, so I asked my lyricist friend, Muriel Robinson, to write words for a song about the feeling of freedom that comes from controlling a car. Composer Jeff Waxman produced a theme in less than five minutes on his trusty synthesizer, where he later composed the rest of the score. We tried various child singers but struck out because there was an epidemic of flu. So finally Jeff's girlfriend, Lisa, tried singing the song. I asked her to sing in a flat and thin voice, without a warble, and she sounded exactly like a young boy.

Extra Expenses

If it were up to me, shooting with a crew I trusted, I would not take out insurance. But if you try to shoot in New York City with the help of the N.Y.C. Mayor's Film Office or in Washington, D.C. with the Washington, D.C. Film Commission, you need at least a million dollars' worth of liability insurance. My premiums would have been lower if we hadn't revealed the near-accident scene. The mere mention of a seven-year-old at the wheel of a limo sent rates soaring, even though I insisted that a kid driving was an illusion we were creating, not a reality. We never did get insurance quotes until the day before shooting. In addition to liability insurance, we needed Workman's Compensation insurance since we were working with SAG actors.

The longer the lead time you have in preparing your film, the more money you can save. As shooting draws nigh, you will be more pressed to spend to keep to the schedule. For example I had to pay double the lab charges to get my answer print finished in time to send it off to Los Angeles in order to qualify for the Oscars. At this point in time, I could use the extra money I spent to give to creditors.

In rating my performance in filming *Jonathan's Turn*, I gave myself a D for fiscal control because the original budget of $15,000 was doubled. Without the economy-mindedness of associate producer Leslie Holland, a Wharton graduate, it would have tripled. As for rating the film, I am going to pass. I think other people have to say it is good. I cannot. I tried to elaborate a kernel of truth and can only hope that other people like it.

16

Postproduction

FILM WORKS BY JUXTAPOSITION. Coming up with the best order and length of shots is discovered by the experience of cutting. In this chapter, the emphasis is not on editorial technique (see appendix III for books on editing), but rather on the emotional experience of being in the cutting room—what this means to the filmmaker and, ultimately, to the audience. I also cover some other basic concerns during postproduction, including music, optical effects, and lab services.

The Power and Process of Editing

Filmmakers have been creating movies from juxtaposing camera shots ever since D. W. Griffith and the Russian pioneers came up with the montage approach to the cinema. Early on, Russian filmmaker and theorist Lev Kuleshov performed an experiment in which he edited scenes of a woman making up before a mirror. The audience had the illusion that they were seeing a woman, but actually she did not exist. Kuleshov used the legs of one woman, the lips of another, the eyes of a third, and the back of a fourth.

In another Kuleshov experiment, he did one reaction shot of an actor playing a prisoner anticipating a bowl of soup; then another of the prisoner looking at the sun, about to be freed. He intercut the prisoner with the soup and with the sun and then transposed the close-ups. No one, not even the actor, could tell which close-up was which. The description of the experiment is widely misquoted but always serves the same purpose: It proves the power of editing. Kuleshov called his method of filmmaking "brick by brick," meaning that he believed in the ensemble, the cumulative impression of pieces of film.

Let's consider your own experience in the cutting room, where you confront what it is you are trying to make the audience know and feel about your story. You start with rushes (or dailies, the screening of your unedited footage), which can often be disappointing because they seem to be only a fraction of what was happening during shooting. What you thought was a lively, vital scene seems dead on the screen. A beautiful face begins to pall. Humor falls flat. Uncut film can be depressing, even when you fast-forward past the bad takes, using your script clerk's notes.

But editing will redeem your film because you have been looking at raw scenes, unpaced by cutting. Once you begin to cut the first scene, your spirits lift. Every cut to a close-up seems to energize the dialogue. The jokes start to work once the gag is paced, constructed anew, and paid off with reaction shots.

Listen to the feelings that you get watching your footage on the Moviola or Steenbeck. If you get depressed or if your stomach tightens, turn up the volume of these twinges and listen to what your body is telling you about your film. You are now in the cutting room and you can try to define those nameless feelings that knock on the door of your conscious critical process. You can *do* something about the actor you've fallen out of love with—if necessary, you can put his or her lines over the person he is talking to. You can even do something about that out-of-focus shot by substituting another scene.

Once you have completed your rough assembly—that is, you have put the selected takes in script order—you start to drop in your closer shots, and after several days you have your rough cut. Aim for two cut minutes a day. This process moves faster in Hollywood, where it is possible to cut nine or ten minutes a day.

A sitcom is often cut on an editing machine called a synchronizer. When I directed an episode of the TV series *The Farmer's Daughter*, editor Ase Clark knew from experience when he wanted a close-up and how long a pause he wanted between the group shot and the close-up. On the synchronizer, he would mark the frame on which dialogue ends, count a few frames, and make the cut. The first time he saw the film at speed was when he passed the rough assembly through the Moviola. If the star, Inger Stevens, looked tired in the assembly, he would immediately look at all the other takes to see if he could get her looking fresher.

Remember that shorts should be short. Cutting is painful but necessary—the fact is that the audience gets the point very quickly. I remember every shot in my short *Happy Birthday to Me* that I was forced to take out thirty years ago, but I'm glad I did the cutting.

When Adam Davidson was working on *The Lunch Date*, a poignant short referred to earlier, Ralph Rosenblum was his editing professor at Columbia University. As Rosenblum recalls, the film started out running nearly half an hour. Rosenblum never said what or where to cut. He simply pointed out where the narrative line was. Originally, this story of an accidental encounter between a homeless man and a suburban woman in a train station had a lot to do with the condition of the homeless. But Rosenblum influenced Davidson to reduce the documentary observations about the homeless and concentrate on the essence of the story. He believes that shorts work best if there is *one incident*. Eventually, pared down to eleven minutes, the film won the top prize for shorts at Cannes and an Academy Award. Probably both honors would have eluded the film in its longer form with a dual focus.

Getting Feedback

Many people take a year to finish their first film. Other people come along and boast that they can do it faster. But you rush to finish a short at your own peril. It takes time to get the right people in to see and critique your film, to think about their comments, to make changes, show it to other people, listen carefully to their feedback. If you are showing your film in front of a group of strangers, there are two ways to go about getting reactions.

The first was told to me by George Stoney, a superb filmmaker who now teaches at New York University. He said that when the film is over, you should just turn on the lights and remain silent. You may have to sit in silence for a while, but eventually one person will speak. When that person is through, another will join in, then another will take exception to the first comment, and the discussion is rolling. Your job is to disappear into the woodwork, listening intently, displaying no sign of vulnerability that could inhibit feedback.

The second way to obtain feedback is by giving people a form to fill out. I used such a form with my film *Teedie* on the childhood of Theodore Roosevelt. The story is about how young Theodore Roosevelt, a skinny, asthmatic, unathletic kid, became a boxer and extroverted politician. When I showed this film to a group of children who were the same age as the intended audience, I tried to make it easy for them to bash the film. I gave every kid a form asking what he or she liked and did not like; whether the film was familiar, believable, slow, fast, understandable, and so forth. I also invited a children's-television producer to look at it. His reaction was to emphasize that he tried to make programs that were *for* children, not just directed *at* children.

The children who watched *Teedie* had questions about pacing, and we identified cuts and passages that needed to be speeded up. Their questions about TR indicated that the film required narration. At the same time, judging from audience reaction, I decided that my film was aimed *at* children instead of being *for* them. I started to write some narration by the child, Teedie, so that the story was told from a child to other children rather than didactically. I used actual quotes from TR's recollection of his childhood, which were found for me by TR's Pulitzer Prize–winning biographer, Edmund Morris, who had been acting as my consultant. I combined the historic quotes with other lines in TR's style.

Then I screened the film for Ralph Rosenblum, the editor who helped Adam Davidson with *The Lunch Date* and who has been a valuable consultant on troubled pictures for several decades. The coauthor of *When the Shooting Stops*, Rosenblum has frequently taken unreleasable movies and has made them marketable with editorial and music changes. After viewing *Teedie*, Rosenblum said that kids needed to be sold more on why they should be interested in TR. He suggested a montage of his achievments. We then assembled such a montage and had it narrated by an imitator of the adult TR, who would not have been the least bit timid in boasting of his achievements. My researcher, Sydney Johnson, got an actual recording of TR's high-pitched, clipped, almost British voice, which the narrator, actor Bob Gunton, imitated.

Once I asked Rosenblum to come to my cutting room to look at one of my quit-smoking shorts. This one was about a man (played by actor-writer-director F. J. O'Neil) who rents a car with his son (played by my son, Jeremy Levy) but does not want to use a seat belt despite the urging of the manager of the rental office. He systematically tries seven different stratagems to deceive the seat belt—tying the belt to the door, lifting the hood to disarm the alarm, climbing from the backseat to the front in case opening the door set off the alarm mechanism, and so on. Finally, the little boy says that he is going to a lot of trouble to keep from saving his life. When this irony is pointed out to him, he concedes, buckles his seat belt, and proceeds to light up a cigarette. We then freeze-frame on the man, who recognizes self-destructive behavior but also is in the grips of the habit.

The problem I asked Rosenblum to address was my gut feeling that the film was amusing but not quite funny enough; in fact, it was rather plodding. Rosenblum said the problem seemed to be that the man was too sane. He should start out sane and become an obsessed madman. Rosenblum also suggested that we ignore the dialogue and create a montage of the action highlights of all the takes, cutting the film to a tempo set by some madcap music. This suggestion inspired my editor, J. J. Linsalata, to rush to a stock music studio. He selected a zany piece of music and recut the piece overnight. In arranging scenes, he followed the music rather than the script, mixed up the intended order of scenes. He made the leading man look increasingly frantic and the little boy increasingly frustrated with his father. The sanity of the rough cut was gone. Picture and music worked together joyously in a picture that escalated in suspense and laughter.

Music

If you are going to score your film with any kind of prerecorded music, you will have to pay royalties to the Musicians Union, ASCAP, or BMI if the film goes into commercial release in the United States or in England. The way to circumvent these charges is to use a recording made in Eastern Europe, which will not be monitored. Jeremy Arnold, who made *On the Lake* as a Wesleyan student, used a British recording for his music. After a long, nagging correspondence with the BBC orchestra, he ultimately had to pay a small fee. The other thing you can do is to go to a music library and select tapes of stock music, which cost a flat fee per use.

As an alternative to prerecorded music, see if you can get friends to compose and/or record your score. Sometimes a single piano, guitar, or flute can be used effectively to score your film. Or ask a music student to do the scoring with a synthesizer.

When I used to work with a composer, the first thing we would do is have a spotting session to decide where music would come in and what it would say. Then I would review the first draft of the composer's piano score, the score would be arranged, musicians would be hired, and the frantic composer would try to record it in three hours, the union minimum. All this changed when I started working with Jeff Waxman on the synthesizer. We can add and subtract instruments, play with the fullness of the sound, and can change it in minutes if it comes out wrong. We can also play it against the film on a TV monitor until we get it right. An acoustic recording sounds better, but who can resist the price and speed of the synthesizer?

Opticals

In 16mm film production, opticals—effects like slow motion, freezes, and credit crawls—have been gradually declining in quality and rising in cost. For the best results, the optical house usually will want to blow up the images to 35mm (for better control) and then reduce them to 16mm for the film. The parsimonious short-maker is probably less interested in skip-printing (using every other frame), slowing down the image (slomo-ing), or superimpositions than in figuring out how to do the credits and acknowledgments. They can be done optically, but for a student film it is better to borrow a computer printer with a choice of fonts. Print a continuous list of credits, then get them photostatted so you have white credits on a black background. To shoot the credits, mount the photostat on an easel and slowly tilt the camera down. Or splurge and send them to an optical service.

Working with the Labs

If you are a student or beginning filmmaker who is shooting with 16mm or 35mm film, you will find that there is a wide variation in the kind of service that labs offer. Some take the attitude that they are courting future clients. They are generous with their time, conducting tours of their facilities, and are patient with the filmmaker's curiosity about timing, fades, dissolves, and so forth. If your lab is stingy with service and information, switch to another one. You need a friendly lab contact. If your workprint (the rushes or first print back from the lab) is bleached or looks blue or warm (reddish), call your contact and talk about the problem. He or she will probably advise you to order a timed workprint. Timing refers to the number of the light that the lab uses to print a given scene. (In general, the numbers range from one to twenty-one.) If the film is exposed normally, the eleven light should give you a pleasing result. If you are shooting in 16mm and you want a scene reprinted, you will have to have the whole roll redone; in 35mm, you can have an individual scene redone.

Directing a film is not like working from a manual. It is an adventure, particularly in the proving ground of the editing room, where you have to confront what you actually filmed rather than what you intended to shoot. The cutting room is a place to face your problems unflinchingly and to come up with creative solutions.

Technological change is a constant in film and video. One of the latest changes has to do with the availability of 8mm portable cameras. The idea of being able to get a usable image with a camera weighing only a few pounds is awesome to someone who started out when the speed of film was 10 and 25 ASA and you had to pour lights on your subject and set; when you had to carry around a half ton of equipment in a station wagon in order to shoot with a minimum crew of four; when it required two hours of set-up from arrival at location until the first shot. As with many innovations, however, these new cameras bring both new short-cuts and new problems.

17

███████████████

Hi-8 and
Super VHS
Cameras

THE FIRST TIME I SAW A HOME VIDEO was in 1988. I watched the
tape with a student of mine, Amanda Fillipachi, who had just
received a video camera as a birthday present from her parents.
From the backseat of a car, she had photographed her mother
driving her brother to the train station and going over with him
what he should know about the people who would be meeting his
train. I watched hypnotically with all my viewer instincts. I
wanted to see the next scene. The camera convinced me that a
story was starting.

In a couple of years, the half-inch (VHS) and 8mm formats
really caught on. Soon *America's Funniest Home Videos* was the
number one show on TV. I have heard of several features shot with
a Hi-8 camera—which produces the best image of all the video
cameras—and Francis Ford Coppola, in his wife's documentary
Hearts of Darkness, foresees a time when a young girl in the
Midwest will pick up her father's camera and make a stunning
work of art.

To date (1993), seventeen million people in the United States have purchased video cameras. After you shoot, if you are headed for film festivals, the challenge is to maintain picture quality. (The list of film festivals in appendix I does not include those amateur festivals that will accept shorts with low-quality images and high-quality stories and production.) The recent excitement over the Hi-8 camera is based on its lightness and portability and its close-to-professional image on the screen.

The Hi-8 Camera

At the present time, Sony is the only manufacturer of the Hi-8 camera. (The most popular model is the Sony 9100.) This camera is easy to use, but there are some problems with getting a good image on the screen. The first one is video noise or visual static, the buildup of grain when the color breaks up. This happens when you shoot people wearing bright colors in poor light conditions or when you boost the gain electronically, which is like "pushing" in film development.

The second problem is color deterioration—fading of color saturation. This can be minimized by using a time-base corrector when you transfer tape. If you edit with a Sony EVO-9700, the machine will automatically compensate to minimize color and detail loss when making dub.

The third problem is dropouts—missing frames of sound and picture. A dropout, sometimes called "catastrophic dropout," can take the form of no picture and no sound or it can consist of strange, unwelcome shapes intruding into your picture. Dropouts are caused by dirt specks getting sucked into the tape by the static electricity generated as you shoot. Currently, there are efforts under way to change the tape shell—the plastic container—by building in an antistatic component. If they are successful, a major problem will be solved without making your equipment obsolete. But your battle with dirt will not be over. Using a cleaning tape in the camera and the editing machine is a start, but it is not enough. Every two weeks or so, you must clean the heads of your camera and any editing machine you use with a dry cloth or with a detergent-soaked cloth, if necessary.

Currently, the Sony 9100 Hi-8 picture has 425 lines of horizontal resolution. Home TV sets have a capacity of 425–450. After editing, you can make a dubbing master, which will retain 75 percent of the original lines. For a better-quality image, there is a new three-chip camera, which has 725 lines. It costs $8,000 and rents for $80 per day.

The Super VHS Camera

The alternative to Hi-8 is Super VHS, which also has 425 lines of resolution. There will be fewer dropouts with VHS because the same speck of dirt will be only a third as large on the image as it is on the Hi-8 equipment. Editing equipment is less than half the price of that for Hi-8, but it is *not* frame accurate. At this writing, the leading brand of editing machine could be off by two to six frames, which means you cannot have professional finesse. While tape costs are comparable, the Super VHS camera is considerably heavier than the Hi-8. You have to decide for yourself how heavy a camera you can carry around efficiently. When I interviewed Scooter McCrae of CTL Electronics in New York, where I bought my own Hi-8 equipment, he admitted a personal preference for VHS with its half-inch format. But since the industry is refining 8mm faster than VHS, he recommends buying into Hi-8.

Types of Tape

When you are purchasing stock for your short, shop around for the best-quality tape. At the moment, Sony does not make the best quality, but this is subject to change without notice. The so-called evaporated metal tape produces a better image with less video noise than the metal particle tape. On the other hand, the evaporated metal tape begins to flake faster than the metal particle tape, which is best used for dubs and editing.

Editing on the Sony EVO-9700

Although the preferred way to edit is to transfer your original tape to a larger format, such as three-quarter-inch or Beta SP, you can save money by editing in 8mm with a Sony EVO-9700. There are cheaper machines, but only the Sony machine is frame accurate. My advice would be to borrow or to rent this machine, unless you intend to use it often. You will generally pay 1 percent of the purchase price to rent the machine for a day.

Here's how the Sony Hi-8 EVO-9700 works. On the left is the player side, which has a slot for your unedited tape. (The machine accommodates both 8mm and Hi-8 tape.) Since you are going to be running this tape and are thus inviting dropouts, it should be a dub of your original. On the right is the recorder side, where you insert a blank tape onto which you will transfer the scenes that you decide to use for the final edit. Let us assume that you have already made your paper cut and have been entering your decisions into the machine's computer by giving the code numbers of the beginning and end of each scene.

To insert a scene for a reel you are building, you first go to your "in" point (first usable frame) by speeding to the right frame with your jog dial, the wheel that enables you to speed up or slow down the tape movement. Go forward until the first usable frame. Then set the recorder side to the last usable frame of the scene you have transferred. Put both sides on pause mode. Set the machine in program mode with the beginning and end points indicated, then push the preview button. Both tapes will back up exactly three seconds for "preroll," go forward at speed, and then execute the trial edit. Reset the machine to edit, and this time the machine's computer will record the information on its own decision list. It can store up to ninety-nine edit decisions.

Before you begin to edit, make an 8mm dub with a window time code which you can use in making your on-line edit into a three-quarter-inch or one-inch dubbing master. If you want to finish in Hi-8, you can use the numbers automatically encoded in your original when you shoot. You will need these numbers when you make your edit decision list either on paper or in a computer attached to the editing machine.

Of course, editing is a process of trying and revising. You can shorten and lengthen scenes by putting the machine in the program mode and changing the edit decisions in the computer. If you want to change shot 12, for example, you can keep your other editing decisions and insert the change, giving the computer the new code numbers. In order to view the change, however, you have to execute it, change any other decisions you want to revise, and ask the computer to make you a new viewing tape. You can also program the machine to eliminate shot 12 and to place it later. The machine will then automatically move the data for shot 13 into instructions for shot 12.

You can use this same machine to do your sound editing and even a mix. In summary, I advise you to buy an 8mm camera if you will use it frequently and become proficient. But you will probably not use the editing machine very often so there is no advantage in owning it if you can borrow or rent.

The video camera opens up a world of possibilities for the filmmaker. It eliminates a big crew and bulky equipment. It gives the writer-director the option to be the cinematographer in some, maybe not all, situations. It is like an animation pencil test, a chance to test your story and the actors' performances with little risk. For documentaries, where picture quality may take second place to content, it is a way of making a film without the tedium of fund-raising.

In the end, however, the audience does not care what type of equipment you use. The audience wants an emotional experience, whether it is shot on film, on Hi-8, or on VHS. The audience cares about characters and a story. It acknowledges beauty in photography, excellence in acting, decor and scenery. But these are not enough. Your obligation is to put your very best story on the screen—to create a short that is totally yours—your own truth, presented in a way that wins an audience. Think of yourself as a molder of ideas, someone who can enlighten us with something you uniquely perceive as true and entertaining. Think of yourself as someone who can pierce through the fog that obscures the truth of human situations and show them in new and clear ways; someone who can help us understand the world around us—as Balzac put it, that universal "human comedy."

Appendix I

Festivals

ENTERING YOUR SHORT IN FESTIVALS CAN BE FUN. It gives you a chance to travel, meet people, get feedback on your short, receive praise and applause, see cutting-edge films. The flip side is that you may have to harden yourself to criticism, both relevant and irrelevant, valid or invalid. You may hear from very vocal critics who represent political minorities and see the world through a narrow prism. Feeling the pain that they feel will increase your humanity even though they do not address your concerns about your film. You should have with you a package of publicity materials for your short, which includes information on how to reach you, stills from the short, a plot summary, your biography and filmography, a list of festival prizes you've won, quotes from notables who have seen your film, and any other ammunition you can find.

When your film is being screened, you may want to sit in the back row to see whether the audience laughs, applauds, or walks out. Bear in mind that people get somewhat jaded from watching a long string of films at a festival, so reactions may be muted. But

251

if you are asked to take a bow, this is when you should flash a smile so your face can be linked with your film. You may meet your next collaborator at the bar later. Or someone with money may express interest in your film tomorrow or the next day. Remember that people who walk out do not necessarily dislike your film. Distributors may leave your screening to dash to other screenings. Perhaps they have made note of your film and intend to order it to see later at their leisure. Avoid the temptation to leave the festival— the participants tend to wax friendlier as the event draws to a close.

The following list includes domestic festivals that have had favorable reports through the years, amateur festivals here and abroad, and festivals in this country that offer cash prizes. To reach festivals overseas, you should submit your film to CINE— Council on International Nontheatrical Events, 1001 Connecticut Avenue NW, Suite 1016, Washington, DC 20036. CINE, which represents the United States Information Agency, will enter your film for you, but you are still free to enter overseas festivals on your own.

There are two sources of book-length compilations of festivals: You can get one from CINE by writing to the above address; AIVF (Association of Independent Video and Filmmakers), at 625 Broadway, New York, NY 10012, also distributes a book, entitled *AIVF Guide to International Film and Video Festivals.*

Even though some of the festivals listed cater to the amateur, if it is your first film, why not enter? Maybe you will be called a promising professional at the next festival.

International Film Festivals

Czechoslovakia

BRNO SIXTEENTH INTERNATIONAL AMATEUR FILM
  FESTIVAL—October
Mestske Kulturni Stredisko
Dum U Dobreho Pastyre-B16Radnicka 4,
65635 Brno, CZECHOSLOVAKIA
Phone: 23925-9

France

WATTRELOS SHORT FILM AND VIDEO FESTIVAL—
  November
140 Rue Faidherbe
59150 Wattrelos, FRANCE
Phone: 20 75 86 46

Germany

INTERNATIONAL SHORT FILM FESTIVAL, OBER-
  HAUSEN—April–May
Christian-Steger-Str. 10
D-4200 Oberhausen 1, GERMANY
Phone: (0208) 825 2652/2420/807008
AWARDS: Cash prizes of 1–1,000 deutsche marks

INTERNATIONALE DUISBURGER AMATEUR FILTAGE
  & VIDEO FORUM—June
Welkerstrasse 4
D-4100 Duisburg 1, GERMANY
Phone: 0203/29477
ELIGIBILITY: Amateur filmmakers under thirty

Italy

FESTIVAL INTERNAZIONALE CINEMA GIOVANI—
 November
Piazza San Carlo 161
10123 Turin, Italy
Phone: 39/11 547171
Fax: 39/11 519796

Spain

III BEINAL NACIONAL CAJALICANTE DE CINE
AMATEUR DE LIBRE CREACION—March
No. 41, 3a Planta
Alicante, SPAIN
Phone: 5206544-5219556

CERTAMEN INTERNACIONAL DE CINE AMATEUR—
 October
"CIUTAT D'IGUALADA"
Apartado 378, 08700 Igualada
Barcelona, SPAIN
Phone: 34 3 804 69 07
Fax: 34 3 804 43 62
CATEGORIES: Fiction, animation, documentary
AWARDS: Grand Prize to the best film at the festival, first
 and second prizes awarded in each category for each format,
 first and second prizes in Category B

CERTAMEN INTERNACIONAL DE VIDEO—December
Cineocho-Optica Tena
C/El Pozo 3
44001 Teruel, SPAIN
Phone: 974 60 00 12

CATEGORIES: Fiction, animation, documentary, experimental

CONCURSO DE CINE AMATEUR—October
Plaza de Valencia
7 Quart de Poblet (Valencia), SPAIN

CONCURSO NACIONAL DE CINE AMATEUR—February
Plaza de Espana, 9 Escalera Dcha. 10 Izda.
28008 Madrid, SPAIN
Phone: 91-247982

MUESTRA DE CINE INTERNACIONAL—October
Apartado de Correos 194
11480 Jerez De La Frontera, SPAIN
Phone: 956-33 53 17

SEMANA DE CINE AMATEUR DEL PAIS VASCO
Casa de la Cultura. C/ Paseo de la Florida s/n
01005 Vitoria Gasteiz, SPAIN
Phone: 945-134405

Tunisia
FESTIVAL INTERNATIONAL DU FILM AMATEUR DE
    KELIBIA—July–August
P.O. Box 116
1015 Tunis, TUNISIA
Phone: (01) 280.298216.1.348.824
AWARDS: Gold, silver, and bronze falcons, jury prizes

U.S. Film Festivals

California
AMERICAN FILM INSTITUTE
LOS ANGELES INTERNATIONAL FILM FESTIVAL—April
2021 North Western Ave.
Los Angeles, CA 90027
Phone: 213-856-7707
Fax: 213-462-4049
ELIGIBILITY: Works not previously shown in L.A.
DEADLINE: Mid-January; shorts (under 60 min.), mid-
  December

ANNUAL VISIONS OF THE U.S. VIDEO CONTEST—
  August
The American Film Institute
2021 North Western Ave.
Los Angeles, CA 90027
Phone: 213-856-7787
ELIGIBILITY: Noncommercial videos not to exceed 20 min.
CATEGORIES: Fiction, nonfiction, experimental, music video

SAN FRANCISCO ART INSTITUTE FILM FESTIVAL—April
Film Festival Committee
800 Chestnut St.
San Francisco, CA 94133
Phone: 415-771-7020, ext. 53
ELIGIBILITY: No longer than 30 min.
Awards: $800 cash; other smaller cash prizes

Colorado
ASPEN FILM FESTIVAL—September
Aspen Filmfest
P.O. Box 8910
Aspen, CO 81612
Phone: 303-925-6882
ELIGIBILITY: Independent work completed from January of
the previous year
CATEGORIES: Feature, documentary, short subject
AWARDS: $2,300 in cash prizes

District of Columbia
WOMEN MAKE MOVIES—March
P.O. Box 19272
Washington, DC 20036
Phone: 202-232-2254

Florida
CENTRAL FLORIDA AMATEUR FILM AND VIDEO
FESTIVAL—April
c/o The Association of Cinematic and Video Arts
P.O. Box 536202
Orlando, FL 32853
Phone: 407-678-1841
CATEGORIES: Comedy, documentary, drama, science fiction,
animation, experimental, nature

Massachusetts
NEW ENGLAND FILM AND VIDEO FESTIVAL—May
Arts Extension Service
Division of Continuing Education, Goodell Bldg.
University of Massachusetts
Amherst, MA 01003
Phone: 413-545-2360
Fax: 413-545-3405
ELIGIBILITY: Works completed within past two years that are
under 60 min.; entrants must be residents of New England or
attend school there
CATEGORIES: Independent and student
AWARDS: Over $5,000 in cash and service awards
DEADLINE: Independents and students, early February
ENTRY FEE: Independents, $30; students, $20. Maximum of
two entries
FORMAT REQ.: 16mm, Hi-8, three-quarter-inch, half-inch
video

New Jersey
THOMAS A. EDISON BLACK MARIA FILM VIDEO
FESTIVAL—January
c/o Jersey City State College
Dept. of Media Arts
203 West Side Ave.
Jersey City, NJ 07305
Phone: 201-200-2043
AWARDS: Cash prizes and certificates
DEADLINE: Mid-November

New York
ANNUAL INDEPENDENT FEATURE FILM MARKET—
  September–October
132 West 21st St., 6th fl.
New York, NY 10011
Phone: 212-243-7777
ELIGIBILITY: Films completed since the previous October 1
DEADLINE: Mid-July
FORMAT REQ.:   VHS preselection, 35/16mm film

ANNUAL ROCHESTER INTERNATIONAL AMATEUR
  FILM FESTIVAL—May
Box 17746
Rochester, NY 14617
Phone: 716-288-5607 (evenings)
DEADLINE: Early March

NATIONAL STUDENT MEDIA ARTS EXHIBITION—
  September
Student Exhibition Committee
Visual Studies Workshop
31 Prince St.
Rochester, NY 14607
ELIGIBILITY: Works by students in grades K-12, colleges,
  and universities (undergraduate and graduate levels)
AWARDS: Month-long exhibition at Visual Studies Gallery
DEADLINE: Late June
FORMAT REQ.:   three-quarter-inch VHS, Beta, Hi-8 video

NEW DIRECTORS/NEW FILMS—March
The Film Society of Lincoln Center
140 West 65th St.
New York, NY
Phone: 212-877-1800, ext. 489

NEW YORK EXPO OF SHORT FILM & VIDEO—November
The New School
Media Studies Dept.
66 West 12th St.
New York, NY 10011
Phone: 212-505-7742
ELIGIBILITY: Noncommercial works, less than 60 min.
CATEGORIES: Animated, feature, experimental, documentary
AWARDS: First, second, third prize in each category
DEADLINE: Early September
FORMAT REQ.:   16mm film, three-quarter-inch video (VHS
   for previewing only)

North Carolina
CHARLOTTE FILM AND VIDEO FESTIVAL
Mint Museum of Art
2730 Randolph Road
Charlotte, NC 20207
Phone: 704-337-2000
ELIGIBILITY: Must be a resident of the southern United States
CATEGORIES: Documentary, narrative, experimental, ani-
   mated, short, and feature films
AWARDS: $3,500 in cash prizes and various in-kind awards
DEADLINE: Early March

Ohio
ATHENS INTERNATIONAL FILM & VIDEO FESTIVAL—
  April–May
75 West Union St., Rm. 407
Columbus, OH 45701
Phone: 614-593-1330
CATEGORIES: Short and feature experimental, documentary,
  narrative, and animated works
DEADLINE: Film, early March; video, early February

Oregon
PORTLAND INTERNATIONAL FILM FESTIVAL—
  February–March
Northwest Film Study Center
Oregon Art Institute
1219 Southwest Park Ave.
Portland, OR 97205
Phone: 503-221-1156
ELIGIBILITY: Invitational
AWARDS: Best of festival
DEADLINE: December

Pennsylvania
BUCKS COUNTY FILM FESTIVAL—November
c/o Smith & Toner
8 East Court St.
Doylestown, PA 18901
Phone: 215-348-3588
ELIGIBILITY: Short and independent film
AWARDS: $2,500, $3,000 in rental fees
FORMAT REQ.:   16mm film

Texas
HOUSTON INTERNATIONAL FILM & VIDEO
   FESTIVAL—April
P.O. Box 56566
Houston, TX 77256
Phone: 713-965-9955
ELIGIBILITY: Films and videos completed no more than two
   years prior to festival
CATEGORIES: Short, documentary, feature, experimental,
   TV commercial, TV production, student, music video, scrips,
   new media, film market, others
AWARDS: Grand prizes, best of category, gold, silver, bronze
   awards, cash prizes for students
FORMAT REQ.:   16/35mm film (magnetic or optical), three-
   quarter-inch and half-inch VHS, NTSC, no Beta

Appendix II

Selected
Shorts

CURRENTLY, there is no one definitive list of shorts. My own list of favorites that follows is the result of years of personal viewing along with suggestions from Richard Ross, former head of the Graduate School at New York University, from people at Tapestry International, Coe Films, Phoenix Films, American Film Institute, and others.

If you would like to view one of the shorts I describe, try to find it at your public library. Many libraries have a collection of cassettes that can be taken out, or have a viewing room to watch the films there. If you cannot find the short at the library, you can write to the distributor that is listed. The distributor may be helpful in telling you where you can obtain the film; it probably will be pleased to sell you a cassette but reluctant to rent one to you.

When I know that one of the shorts on this list is out of circulation, I have given a lengthier description of the plot. I hope that even if you cannot watch some of these shorts, you will at least see the imaginative premises of the filmmakers.

Aisle Six

In this innovative satire on the power of conformity, high school priorities are scrambled so that girls swoon over plumbers instead of football players. The story tracks one nonconformist who shocks everyone with his aspiration to attend MIT to become an electrical engineer. Directed by David Wain. Not distributed.

The Bet

An addictive gambler risks his half of the deli business he co-owns with his brother. He deceives his brother and himself but cannot fool the mob. Directed by Ted Demme. In an anthology packaged by Films By Edmond Levy.

Birch Street Gym

Jack is idling away his senior years playing chess in an old-age home. Suddenly, he joins a gym that caters to seniors. Boxing gives them an occasional black eye but also a reason to live. Directed by Stephen Kessler, written by him and Mark Wilkins. Produced and distributed by Chanticleer Films.

Board and Care

Lila, a teenager with Down's Syndrome, needs a boyfriend. At a picnic, she meets Richie and they fall in love but are separated and pine for each other. Oscar winner. Writer-director Ron Ellis dedicates this film to his sister, Laura Jean Ellis, who was born with Down's Syndrome. Distributed by Coe Film Associates. It is also in an anthology packaged by Films By Edmond Levy.

A Chairy Tale

A chair takes on a life of its own, teasing and tormenting a man who wants to sit down by continuously eluding him. When he decides to spurn the chair, it pays court to him. Made by the preeminent experimental filmmaker Norman McClaren. Distributed by the National Film Board of Canada.

Chapparal Prince

Lena, a teenage runaway working as a kitchen slave, writes a despairing letter to her mother. The mail stagecoach is attacked and robbed, but Lena's letter is read by a sensitive robber who comes to her rescue. From a story by O. Henry, directed by Herbert Spencer. Distributed by Coronet MTI Film and Video.

The Chicken

In this nearly wordless film, a boy adopts a chicken that his parents bring home for food. Trying to convince the parents not to slaughter it, he steals an egg each day from the refrigerator and puts it under the chicken to prove that the bird should be spared for its egg production. But then the bird crows at dawn. More than anything, this is a portrait of a happy family by French director Claude Berri. Distributed by Coronet MTI Film and Video.

Day of the Painter

A man sits reading the *Wall Street Journal* in a rustic setting on the steps of his cabin. Suddenly aware that he must rouse himself and do some work, he floats a long, narrow board under a bridge. He pours, sprays, shoots paint at the board until it is covered with splotches of color in the manner of Jackson Pollack. When the paint has dried, he saws the wood into separate paintings like sausage links. A dealer lands a seaplane on the lake, selects a half dozen for his gallery, and takes off. A delightful statement about the way some modern art is cynically turned out. Oscar winner. Directed by Ezra Baker. Out of circulation.

Distant Traveller

When a tour bus breaks down in India, a woman passenger goes exploring. She pursues a half-clad figure and a little boy into the jungle to a Hindu temple where she watches a funeral ceremony. She has a fantasy in which she is a Hindu widow consigning her husband to the flames. Directed by David Rathod. Distributed by Coe Film Associates.

The Dove

This parody of an Ingmar Bergman film, made when he was the dominant artistic cinema force in the world, is reminiscent of the master's film *Wild Strawberries* about a professor's return to his roots. The dialogue is a Swedish-accented amalgam of Yiddish and English and subtitles. Written by Sid Davis (who plays Death), directed by Anthony Lover, and produced by George Coe (who plays the professor). Oscar nomination. Distributed by Anthony Lover, Liberty Studios.

End of the Rainbow

A depressed, untalented musician plays badly on his fire escape. Jeered by the crowd below, he jumps to the street. In a fantasy sequence, he staggers to his feet and plays brilliantly in a wild musical number before reality returns. Directed by Lazlo Papas. A winner at the Chicago International Film Festival and Bilboa International Film Festival. Distributed by Tapestry International.

Fifteenth Phase of the Moon

The full moon wreaks changes in this Mexican-American family, propelling it toward American values rather than Hispanic tradition. Directed in a very erotic style by Mark Amos Nealy, who cowrote the script with Celia Roebuck Reed, whose story it was based upon. Produced and distributed by Chanticleer Films.

Graffiti

In an Hispanic city, a graffiti artist plays cat and mouse with authorities, but the game changes when he watches a woman graffiti artist arrested and tortured. Mathew Patrick cowrote the script with Randee Russell and also directed the movie. Distributed by Cinema Guild.

Greasey Lake

TC's cool and antisocial pranks stop when he and his friends drive to Greasey Lake in his mother's car without permission. They clash with a biker, whom they leave for dead. From the story by T. Coraghesson Boyle. Directed by Damian Harris. Distributed by Chanticleer Films.

Halmani

Halmani (Korean for *grandmother*) pays her first visit to her daughter who lives with her American husband and Amerasian daughter in the California desert. There is disillusionment on both sides, but the clashes end up on a positive note. Written and directed by Kyung-Ja Lee through the AFI (American Film Institute). Distributed by Pyramid Films.

With Hands Up

The film takes its departure from one of the most famous shots of World War II, which a Nazi photographer snapped of an eight-year-old child in a newsboy hat with his hands up as Nazis are rounding up Jews. A fantasy correction. Grand prize at Cannes. Directed by Mitko Panov. Distributed by NYU Film School.

How Sticky My Fingers, How Fleet My Feet

Each week some pudgy men in their mid thirties, including a doctor and a foundation executive, play touch football in the park. In choosing up sides, no one wants the sixteen-year-old nephew one man has brought along, but he has a lesson to teach them all on the football field: "If you live long enough you get old." Directed by John Hancock. Nominated for an Oscar. In an anthology packaged by Films By Edmond Levy.

The Howie Rubin Story

Howie has grandiose fantasies of being the subject of an Ed Murrow interview, singing in a nightclub, and getting attention from girls. But real life keeps interrupting when his mother calls to him. Directed by Rod Cohen. Made at the University of Southern California. Not distributed.

In the Name of the Father

In the time of the crusades, an English knight is awakened in the forest by two French children. Without thinking, he kills the girl and then kidnaps the boy, who may be her brother. The film shows the developing relationship between the captor and his captive. Directed by Paul Warner from a screenplay by Paul McCudden through AFI. Distributed by Tapestry International.

Kaboom

A man brings home a nuclear bomb as a novelty fad item. At first his wife is worried, then she treats it like a baby, and soon she and the neighbors all want one of their own. Directed by Gabrielle Luzzi. Distributor unknown.

The Last Days of Hope and Time

Albert Lee, a high school basketball star, washed out of the pros and spends every day on the basketball court instead of working, although his wife needles him to be a better role model to their son. Made at AFI and directed by Andrew Wagner. Distributed by AFI.

The Laureate

The protagonist is a Russian émigré writer, famous at home, but in America his publisher wants to add sex to his prison memoir, and he works as a baby-sitter writing a new novel when he can. Distributed by Tapestry International.

The Lunch Date

A woman goes into a cafeteria while waiting for a train. She puts her coat and packages down, gets herself a salad, puts it on a table, goes to the ladies' room, and returns to find a homeless man eating her salad. She gets another fork, sits down, and without exchanging a word, insists on sharing the salad. After leaving to catch her train, she suddenly remembers her packages. She returns to the cafeteria, finding her packages *and* her salad untouched at another table. Written and directed by Adam Davidson. Distributed by Robert Lantz Office.

Marilyn Hotchkiss's Ballroom Dancing and Charm School

This riotous comedy follows a group of squabbling boys and girls, who are sent to Mrs. Hotchkiss's school kicking and screaming, where they learn to become polished ladies and gentlemen. Made by AFI, written and directed by Randall Miller, who launched his feature career with this film. Distributed by Tapestry International.

Missing Parents

In this spoof of runaway kids and frantic parents, the roles are reversed. Hans has been abandoned by his parents and lives on his own. Finally, Hans finds them at a shelter for runaway parents. Directed by Martin Nicholson. Distributor unknown.

Night Movie

Few words are spoken in this moving story of the relationship between a sensitive Israeli soldier and a young Arab teenager who is his captive. Directed by Gur Heller with excellent cinematography by Jorge Gurvich, accented by excellent music by Oded Jehavi. No U.S. distribution.

An Occurrence at Owl Creek Bridge

Among the most beloved shorts of all time, this Civil War story shows the final fantasies of a man about to be hung. The life he might have had is seen in beautiful slow motion. From a story by Ambrose Bierce. Directed by Robert Enrico. Distributed by Films Inc.

Portrait of Grandpa Doc

This film cross-cuts between a young man's present preparations for an art exhibit and his tender memories of summer days with his grandfather, who first validated his talent and sent him to art school. Written and directed by Randall Kleiser about his own grandfather. Distributed by Phoenix Films.

Proof

Some beer-swilling good old boys drive a "friend" to the office of Pecos Parachute School, where they force him to go up in a rickety plane, not knowing that the pilot's crazy wife switched her laundry with the parachute. When he jumps without a parachute, the boys scream instructions he cannot hear. At the last minute, he saves himself with the safety chute. Written and directed by Kevin Reynolds, who went on to direct *Robin Hood: Prince of Thieves* with Kevin Costner. Made into a feature called *Fandango*. Made and distributed by the University of Southern California.

The Red Balloon

The worldless film classic is a fantasy about a balloon that bonds with a boy, floating behind him as he goes on his way. When a bully punctures the red balloon, other balloons come to the boy's rescue. Written and directed by Albert Lamorisse, this is probably the world's most famous and beloved short. Distributed by Janus Films; also try video stores.

The Room

A boy of ten, held captive in his apartment by a tyrannical father, fantasizes that his bed blasts off from the apartment like a space-ship and lands in the street below where he is warmly greeted by neighbors. Directed by Jeff Balsmeyer and photographed by his brother Randall, the film won the best short film prize in the 1992 Cannes Festival. In an anthology packaged by Films By Edmond Levy.

Sandino Bambino

Martin, good in school but overly serious and idealistic about life, watches his parents split up and his fun-loving father go off with Martin's girlfriend in this funny and poignant rite of passage. Written, directed, and edited by Andrew Humphries at the Royal College of Art. Not distributed.

The Sink

In this silent black-and-white film, we meet a woman who is routinely working at her kitchen one day when something attached to a rope clogs her sink. She keeps tugging on it and finally pulls up a nearly alive miniature man covered with muck, whom she throws in the garbage. Soon the man is sleeping in her bed. It tries to woo her, but she kills it. Ambiguous and haunting. Written and directed by Alison McClean, an American who has lived in New Zealand. Distributed by Andalusian Pictures.

Skater Dater

Visual poetry. Without dialogue, it tells the story of a group of boys, twelve to thirteen years old, who skateboard together in the hills of Venice, California. When one boy collides with a girl, flirts with her, peels from the group and they go off together, he is ostracized and challenged by the other boys to a downhill race while they try to topple him in a contest of dominance. Soon the other boys begin to notice girls and begin their own transition from skater to dater. Written and directed by Noel Black, photographed by Michael Murphy. Distributed by MGM/UA.

Tell Me

Celia, the principal character, and her best friend, Nancy, have vowed to undergo all the stages of adolescence together and to tell each other everything. But Nancy develops breasts first and attracts a boy at the Moonlight Dance while Celia has to listen to an overweight boy make an anti-flat-chested remark. Celia runs out in tears, spotting Nancy making out in a car with a boy. Wanting equality with her, Celia allows the fat boy to kiss her but then cries. Written and directed by Mary Beth Fiedler. Made and distributed by the University of Southern California.

That Burning Question

A journalist, his girlfriend, and a photographer travel by subway to chase down a story of a man threatening suicide. As they travel, we learn that the girlfriend wants a commitment, which is just what the man who threatens suicide wants. If the woman he loves will not take him back, he threatens to douse himself with gasoline and light a match. She relents, but as the couple goes home they are still ambivalent, maybe a tad less so. Written and directed by Alan Taylor, the film was made on a grant from the Mobil Corporation by the Academy of Motion Picture Arts and Sciences. Distributed by Tapestry International.

Time Expired

In this compassionate comedy, Bobby, a working-class man, returns from prison to his dutiful wife with her gossip and his stolid, tiny mother with her shepherd's pie. Unable to start a new life, he lies to his wife and trysts with Ruby, his transvestite cellmate in prison. Bobby tries to straddle two worlds until Ruby wins a showdown with the wife. Written and directed by Danny Leiner. Distributed by Tapestry International.

Walking the Dog

A woman runs an antique store and has a fierce sentimental attachment to all the objects in her store. At the same time she has debts and cannot afford this self-destructive possessiveness. When a teenager comes to rob her, he reminds her of her dead son, a yo-yo champion whose specialty was the trick walking the dog. After she gives him a yo-yo and a chance to earn money, the boy goes straight. This act of trust marks the beginning of her own change; she eventually lets go of her possessions at an auction. Written and directed by Bonnie Paleff. Distributed by Fox Lorber.

Welcome to I.A.

At his own birthday party, no one talks to Paul. It dawns on him that he is having another attack of invisibility. People see through him and ignore what he says. He joins Invisibles Anonymous and gets a book whose central thesis is that when you start seeing other people, they start seeing you. At a meeting later, Paul celebrates thirty days of visibility. An amiable but profound short. Written and directed by Michael Scheff, produced by him and his wife. Distributed by KS Distribution.

The White Mane

The stallion referred to in the title is the most beautiful and proud member of a pack of wild horses that roams free in the wilderness. He fights a challenger who tries to take away his leadership in a long, bloody battle. Eventually, he is captured by ranchers who want to break him and domesticate him. He is freed by children, and he returns to the pack to find that another leader has taken his place. They fight. White Mane loses—but he is free. Directed by the maker of *The Red Balloon*, Albert Lamorisse. Distributed by the University of California Extension.

Distributors Named Above

AFI c/o April Gates
2021 North Western Ave.
P.O. Box 27999
Los Angeles, CA 90027
213-856-7600

Andalusian Pictures
c/o New Zealand Film Commission
Aukland, New Zealand
Fax: 644-384-9719

Chanticleer Films
1680 West Vine St.
Hollywood, CA 90028
213-462-4705

Coe Film Associates
65 East 96th St.
New York, NY 10128
212-831-5355

Coronet MTI Film and Video
108 Wilmot Road
Deerfield, IL 60015
800-855-2853

Films By Edmond Levy, Inc.
135 Central Park West
New York, NY 10023
212-595-7666

Films Inc./PMI
5547 North Ravensworth Ave.
Chicago, IL 60640
800-343-4312
Fax: 312-878-0416

Fox Lorber
419 Park Ave. South
New York, NY 10016
212-689-6777 Fax: 212-689-2526

Janus Films
1 Bridge St.
Irvington, NY 10533
914-591-5500

KS Distribution
10400 Summer Holly Circle
Los Angeles, CA 90077
310-475-6937

Liberty Studios
238 East 26th St.
New York, NY 10011
212-532-1865

MGM/UA
6133 River Rd.
Rosemont, IL 60018
312-518-0500

National Film Board of Canada
1251 Avenue of the Americas
New York, NY 10036
212-596-1770

New York University Film School
721 Broadway
New York, NY 10003
212-998-1803

Phoenix Films
2249 Chaffee Drive
St. Louis, MO 63146
314-569-0211

Pyramid Studio
2801 Colorado Ave.
Santa Monica, CA 90414
310-828-7677

Robert Lantz Office
Att: Dennis Aspland
888 Seventh Avenue
New York, NY 10106
212-586-0200

Swank Motion Pictures
201 S. Jefferson Ave.
St. Louis, MO 63103
800-876-6677

Tapestry International, Inc.
820 Broadway
New York, NY 10010
212-677-6007

University of California Extension
2176 Shattuck Ave.
Berkeley, CA 84704
510-642-6000

Appendix III

Recommended Reading

AT PRESENT, there are no books on shorts that I would recommend, but here are a few good ones on screenwriting and other aspects of filmmaking.

Arijon, Daniel. *Grammar of the Film Language*. Beverly Hills, CA: Silman James Press, 1991.

Coopersmith, Jerome. *Professional Writer's Teleplay/Screenplay Format*. (Available through the Writers Guild East, 555 West 57th St., New York, NY 10019, 212-767-7800.)

Courter, Philip R. *The Filmmaker's Craft: 16mm Cinematography*. Van Nostrand Reinhold, 1982.

Dmytryk, Edward. *On Film Editing*. Stoneham, MA: Focal Press, 1984.

Field, Syd. *Screenplay.* New York: Dell, 1982

Hauge, Michael. *Writing Screenplays that Sell.* New York: McGraw-Hill, 1988.

Holland, Norman. *The Film Editing Room Handbook.* Los Angeles: Lone Eagle, 1990.

Lowell, Ross. *Matters of Light and Depth.* Philadelphia: Broad Street Books, 1992.

Miller, William. *Screenwriting for Narrative Film and Television.* Mamaroneck, NY: Hastings House, 1990.

Reisz, Karel. *Technique of Film Editing.* Stoneham, MA: Focal Press, 1968.

Seger, Linda. *Making a Good Script Great.* Hollywood, CA: Samuel French, 1987.

Index